Greenhorn

– a novel –

Greenhorn

• • •

From Europe to New York City and Beyond, an Immigrant's Adventures in the Roaring Twenties

– a novel –

Pál Királyhegyi

(Paul King)

Anzix Publishing

Published by Anzix Publishing, LLC

First published in 1932, by the Macaulay Company, New York.

Photo by Irén Ács (1924-2015). Courtesy of Hungarian National Museum, Historical Photo Department.

ISBN: 9780999158708
ISBN: 0999158708

Second US edition

10 9 8 7 6 5 4 3 2 1

CHAPTER 1

KLARI WAS FIFTEEN years old. I was eighteen, and I loved her with all my heart. Every moment spent apart from her seemed like a waste of life. It was quite natural that I should play hooky, that morning, so I could go to the zoo and spend the day with her.

The Budapest Zoo is more than a place where one can look at a lot of lonely animals behind iron bars. It is also an important amusement park. There are concerts every day, and many other attractions besides. So as far as I was concerned the greatest attraction was neither in a cage, a tent, nor a side show. It was behind the counter of a soft drink stand. Klari's mother owned the stand, and Klari waited on the customers. When I played hooky, that is where I was to be found.

It had taken an extraordinary amount of courage in the beginning to as much as finish a soft drink in front of the counter, with Klari's eyes behind it. But I had progressed considerably. I had a place behind the counter now, as though by right. I waited on the customers frequently, but what I liked best was to help Klari do so: to hand her jars and glasses, and hope to touch her fingers as objects passed from hand to hand.

"Please give me the strawberry syrup, Paul," said Klari.

"The half-empty jar or a fresh one?" I asked in a whisper.

I liked to talk to her in a low voice. It didn't matter what I said, so long as a private understanding between us was affirmed by conversation others could not hear.

Klari smiled.

"You know very well," she said.

I bent down to get the jar from under the counter. When I straightened up again, my father was looking at me. For a moment, I thought my eyes had played a nasty trick on me. It was eleven in the morning, and he had never, so far as I knew, been inclined to go to the Zoological Garden before. But then I heard his voice, too.

He turned to my frightened mother, who stood beside him. All the shame and sorrow in the world were in his voice:

"I have lived to see the day! Your son is a waiter! A waiter!"

My mother began to weep. My father shouted hoarsely:

"Get out of there! Come over here!"

I was eighteen years old, as I have said, and very conscious of the privileges that should come with that age. Besides, I was standing by the side of the girl I loved. *Certainly,* I thought as I obeyed my father, *I shall not go, since he talks to me like that!*

But I was already standing before him. He grasped my arm firmly. He was a very strong man.

"You . . ." he shouted. But he could say nothing more. He slapped me on the face, twice.

My father slapped my face in public, in the amusement park, in the presence of the girl I loved! And there was nothing I could do. I wished vaguely that the earth might swallow me, knowing very well that the earth is solid and seldom swallows anybody. I thought of the earthquake in San Francisco, years ago. My uncle had been there at the time. But even that had happened in America, which was far from Budapest. If I had not known that it was a womanish thing to do, I should have fainted.

I raised my eyes to look at Klari. Perhaps if I smiled bravely and contemptuously it would ease my shame. Her startled, lovely eyes were fixed on my father's face. He was shaking his finger under her nose and roaring:

"I am his father! It is you who lure him away from school! If I ever see him with you again you'll regret it the rest of your life, you hussy!"

My admiration of Klari increased my shame. She seemed quite cool. After a short pause she said to my father:

"Will you allow me to speak to him for a moment, now?" She did not wait for an answer, but slipped out from behind the counter, took my arm, and led me aside.

"Listen, Paul," she said, "I am very sorry about what has happened. I don't think it is your fault. However, he is your father. And I don't want to have to witness such a scene again. You must promise me not to try to see me again until you are able to take care of yourself."

I still had the jar of strawberry syrup in my hand.

"Here is the strawberry syrup," I said, and handed it to her. "There isn't much in it. . . ."

"No," she said, gauging the amount with her eye, "but we have some more, you know."

"I . . . I . . ."

But my father came over, took me by the arm, and started home. I did not look back.

My mother cried all the way, and no one said a word until we reached home. I scarcely felt the pain anymore. I looked at myself as though from the outside, and it seemed incredible that I was still alive. I walked home like a machine, a hopeless, helpless, stupid little bit of clockwork. Surely I would not live until we reached the door. But I did.

I was eighteen, and I was a nobody. It would be years before I was fit to make my own living. There was no chance of getting work in Hungary. Everything was topsy-turvy, what with the war and all. And I could not see her until I stood on my own feet.

It was perhaps just as well, after all. My father had slapped me twice, publicly and in her presence.

And it would certainly serve no purpose to cry about it now. It had happened. It was the end. There was nothing, absolutely nothing, I could do to regain my self-respect.

There was only one thing to do. I must kill myself. People made a lot of fuss about life and death, when there was really nothing to choose between them, half the time. People talked and thought too much about death, and frightened themselves. That was all. I was not very strong, and would not live very long, anyway.

Was it necessary for my father to have slapped me right there, in front of her?

I would get in touch with Charley Vass, whose father had a big military revolver with heavy bullets. One of those bullets would do the work of a lifetime in less than a second. For what was life but an unnecessarily protracted preliminary to death?

I would explain everything to my friend Charley. He was my best friend, and he would understand perfectly. One sure, deliberate movement, and everything would be finished. Killing oneself was as easy as that.

Greenhorn

I would write no letters. It was silly to write letters before killing oneself. Well, perhaps one long letter to Klari. Nothing to my parents. In that one letter I could explain everything. It would begin like this:

> *When you read these lines, I shall no longer be among the living. . . .*

She would cry, and realize how much I loved her. My parents would cry, too, even my father. He would realize the mistake he made in slapping me—twice, in front of Klari.

The letter would tell her everything—my plans, my hopes, my dreams.

And my father! How frightened he was going to be when he heard the shot, how heartbroken on rushing into my room and finding me lying dead on my bed.

Perhaps it would be still better to go away from home to do it. Let strangers carry home my pale, limp, lifeless body. But first of all I should go to the park once more.

"Goodbye, Klari! I am going far, far away, forever!"

Then I would get Charley's revolver.

I was too young to die! But I had no alternative! Couldn't he have waited until we got home to slap me? Now he had forced me to leave life behind, just when I should be starting life, when I should have plans and dreams and hopes. Poor Klari! How sorry she would be when she found out!

Tomorrow the sun would rise as usual; the streetcars would run as before; the girls would be flirting and laughing on the streets just as they did while I was yet alive. Even Klari would live, and smile. She would smile so sadly, and when someone asked her what made her so sad she would say, with tears in her eyes:

"A man, a good and brave man, died for me."

I decided to put one of my short stories next to my revolver. The newspapers would say that a talented young writer had committed suicide.

My picture would be in the newspapers. Perhaps they would publish the story, too. My father would realize what he had lost, in losing his son, but it would be too late.

I must kill myself. But first I must get the revolver from Charley Vass.

CHAPTER 2

I HAD GREAT respect for Charley Vass. He was tall, strong, and handsome. And he was my best friend. In those days I had no friends, only best friends. I was in a dark mood when I called him up:

"This is Paul speaking. I have something very important to tell you. I must see you where we can talk things over without being disturbed."

Charley talked cheerfully and excitedly:

"I have something very important to tell you, too. I'll see you tonight at the New York Café."

"All right. Tonight at eight o'clock."

Usually it was difficult for me to leave the house after dinner, but no one could have held me back this time. My father was not home in any case.

At the café I sat alone for a few minutes. As I looked into the mirror, a weary, resigned, beaten face looked back at me. The face of a doomed man.

Charley arrived, beaming with happiness and excitement.

"Hello," I greeted him gravely.

"Hello!" he answered cheerfully. Apparently he did not notice my sorrow.

"Gee, Paul, I am so happy. I have great news for you! Two coffees, please."

"With rum," I added. "I have news for you, too. I am going away . . . far, far away. . . ."

"That's just it. That's what I want to do. We'll go together. Now listen. I really don't know how to start. You will scream, Paul, if I tell you. It is about America! We are going there. A strange and marvelous country . . . freedom, liberty, wealth, happiness!"

"Statue of Liberty . . . Woolworth Building. . . ." I remembered.

"Time is money. . . . Rockefeller, Pearl White, J. P. Morgan," he was shouting.

"Cowboys . . . corned beef . . . Edison. . . ."

"Buffalo Bill . . . Nick Carter . . . Rolls Royce. . . ."

"Pinkerton . . . Caruso . . . Prince of Wales. . . ." I was feverish.

"Titanic . . . Business is business. . . ."

"California . . . Greenwich Village. . . ."

And Charley went on:

"We don't want to be slaves of tradition, slaves of our parents, slaves of stupidity anymore! We must go to America! America! God! Tall and impossible buildings, beautiful girls, interesting people, big money. It's a crime to waste another minute here. Are you coming?"

"Of course. We are going! That's why I came here tonight!"

I drank my coffee and ordered another with plenty of rum. But I was worried.

"And the money? We must have money to get there."

"I have a perfect plan, don't worry! We don't' need much. I have everything figured out. We need very little money, about a hundred dollars—I'm figuring in dollars. Trieste,

Italy. . . . There we'll get a job on some steamer, and we'll work our way across."

I was trembling in spite of the rum.

"Great God! And passports?"

"Passports, nothing! Connections! I can take care of that. Passports to Trieste are all we need."

"How glorious! America!"

"Yes, no more rules. . . . New faces . . . new people . . . adventure!"

"Adventure . . . change . . . new hopes . . . new happiness!"

"My father always tells me I have everything I need. He thinks that clothes and food and sleep are everything. We have nothing here, absolutely nothing. We have to do things. We have to become somebodies. Do you understand?"

"Yes, I do. Are you sure we can get enough money? It was hard to believe that it would be so simple.

"Of course. And in case of emergency, we can always go to the Teleky Place."

We left the café together, then we parted.

"I must see a girl tonight yet," said Charley. "Very important."

I walked home alone. That friend of mine, that Charley, was such a nice boy. He must see a girl tonight. He always had important engagements. America! Great! Of course my father would not like it. That did not matter. I was going away. It was fate. Nothing could stop me.

My father always said, "People should die where they are born." He was a very conservative man. If Columbus had listened to him . . . but he hadn't. We were going to America. Charley was wonderful; he was a liar, but he always had good ideas.

I remember little things that had happened during the long years of our friendship. The time he kicked that krone, for example.

He was seven years old then and we went to the same school. He had a krone, a real, shiny krone. Real money! It was strange and unbelievable. Children were given pennies on rare occasions, but kronen? Never! Kronen were for grown–ups only. How could he have a krone? It bothered me all morning in school, and as we walked home, I began to question him about it. Looking bored, he pretended not to notice my admiration and excitement at all.

"We have many of these at home," he said. "Who wants it?"

And he flicked it away! The krone fell to the pavement. I was ashamed to pick it up. Charley began to kick it, and kicked it all the way home. We lived in the same house. I rushed into the house and hid myself, thinking I would wait until he had gone away, and then go out and pick up the precious coin. From my hiding place I could see Charley look around cautiously and then bend down quickly, pick up the krone, and slowly and calmly walk up the stairs without seeing me.

And then later on: the King's visit to their house. Charley made me swear that I would not say a word of it to anybody. It was a deep, dark secret, he said. Terrible things could happen if I didn't keep my promise. It was about the King. The King of Hungary and the Emperor of Austria, who ruled over Austria-Hungary.

"The King was at our house last night," he said. That short statement shook me to the bottom of my heart. I remember the King from the many pictures I had seen of him. Castles, pomp, servants, court, power, the mightiest of all—the King!

I could not say a word. I was dumbfounded. The King! Charley looked around carefully so nobody else should hear the rest of the secret:

"Yes, the King. He came to borrow a sack of kronen from my father. You see, we have many of those sacks at home, and my father has a hiding place, a big cellar. All the guards who watch the money in that cellar are dumb. We bought them with their tongues cut out."

He was excited, too. His eyes were shining. I shivered. To receive the King of Hungary in one's house, to give him a sack of money—there was a father for you!

And when he was about sixteen, he confessed, "Paul, I can't stand it any longer. I must tell you. I can't keep the secret locked in my heart. It started about a month ago, but I didn't want to believe it. I didn't want to notice it. A closed coach followed me every morning when I went to school. An accident, I thought, just an accident, and I didn't pay much attention to it. But four days ago something happened. Something beautiful, Paul. How shall I tell you? The beautiful gilded car suddenly stopped in front of me as I was walking. I looked up and saw a beautiful, blond, pale young girl looking through coach window. We were close to each other. I stopped. She whispered, "Charley, please jump into the coach. Please . . . quickly!" Before I could think, I found myself next to her in the coach, and the driver whipped the horses. 'What is it, beautiful stranger, what can this mean?' I asked the girl.

"She could not answer. She was crying, crying desperately, tears streaming down her lovely cheeks. A few minutes passed. I could hear nothing but the clatter of the horses' hoofs and the sound of her sobbing. I looked through the window and I did not recognize the streets through which our coach was flying. Suddenly she grabbed my arm tightly.

"'Please forgive me and help me,' she implored. 'I am Princess X, (I cannot tell you her real name) and my irate father, the Prince, wants to force me into a marriage with a terrible old archduke, whom I hate. I would rather die than marry him!'

"The princess started to cry again in my arms. I was so surprised and happy that for a while I did not know what to say. I just hugged and caressed her. 'My darling beautiful princess, I love you, too,' I said at last. 'I am ready to die for you, but your rank is too high. Your father would never approve of our marriage. I am but a commoner, how can I marry you?'"

By the time I knew Charley very well, so I interrupted him for a moment:

"Not a word of this is true, is it, Charley?"

"No," he answered, and continued unperturbed:

"'We will go away from this country, my darling Princess. Here we cannot live in happiness. Come with me, dear, far, far away, where we can live for each other.' I could say no more. My heart was filled with love, and with a beautiful, strange happiness I hugged her slender body and kissed her soft, warm lips a million times."

Charley looked away, far away, through the old schoolbuilding, dirty apartment houses, through the sky, through everything. He was thinking of the princess, the beautiful sad princess of his dreams, and I saw tears in his eyes.

Such an unfortunate love affair!

CHAPTER 3

A FEW UNEVENTFUL days passed. My heart continued to throb the same word endlessly: America! America! . . . I felt superior to Budapest and its people. I looked at them as though I were a stranger, a visitor, one whose spirit was already far away, in a greater country, soaring over limitless fields of opportunities. My eyes were full of pity as I looked at streets, buildings, people, as if I were saying: "Goodbye, Budapest, I am sorry, but you are too small for me. Goodbye, people of Budapest, you are nice, but too colorless for me. One-track lives . . . running around in limited circles, while I . . . I am bound for America!"

"Get ready, Paul, we are going to grandfather's house," my mother said one day after dinner.

"What? Another family gathering? I am not going. Relatives bore me. Is it a divorce or a marriage?"

"Didn't you read the paper today? Martin is home. You must come. Grandfather would never forgive you."

"Martin is home? Martin? Of course I am going."

I was going to meet Martin. Marvelous!

Martin was the black sheep of the family, and his name was seldom mentioned. About fifteen years before, at the age of seventeen, he was expelled from school and he went to America. He worked his way there on a ship. We had not heard anything about him since. I picked up the newspaper and found long articles about my American uncle. He was—the paper said—the president of a mining company; he owned a hotel and a bank, and published a Hungarian newspaper about miners. He was a leading Hungarian in America. For once it was worthwhile to go to that hated family gathering.

I have never seen as clannish a family as ours was. They should have lived in biblical times. My grandfather, the chief of the clan, should have been a patriarch. He was ninety years old, with keen eyes and a long white beard. He gathered his enormous family around him on all occasions, whether it was a question of approaching divorce, engagement, dowry for the poor girl in the family, childbirth, or business failure. He had six daughters and four sons. The daughters were married at the age of sixteen and seventeen—he made it his business to marry them off early—so he had dozens of grandchildren, great-grandchildren and great-great-grandchildren. He named all children that were born in the family; he collected money from the rich members of the family when there was a business failure, sickness, or some other calamity; gave gold pieces to good students; and reconciled estranged couples.

Once, a couple separated against Grandfather's wish. Nobody dared tell him, so the couple continued to attend the family gatherings, pretending they lived together happily, to the great joy and satisfaction of Grandfather. After a year, as a result of this compulsory pretense—they changed their minds, made up, and lived together happily ever after. Later on we found out that Grandfather knew of their separation the whole time.

He called the family together now to celebrate the homecoming of a prodigal son, in spite of the fact that Martin had come home successful, and most likely not prodigal at all.

The family gathered in the big dining room of Grandfather's beautiful home. He sat at the head of the table, with Joseph, his oldest and favorite son, on his left, and Martin, the celebrated one, on his right. Everybody was excited, and all talked to Martin at the same time.

"Is it true that people over there eat only canned food?" asked Aunt Fanny. "My doctor son says that isn't good for the stomach."

"Can it be true that girls don't need any dowry there to get married?" asked Uncle Louis, who had a fourteen-year-old daughter.

"Can you tell me something about the famous stockyards in Chicago?" Uncle Joseph asked, for he managed Grandfather's packing house in Budapest.

"Is it true that they move the hundred-story Woolworth Building from one place to another?" inquired Uncle Hugo, who was in the furniture moving business.

"I have heard that they keep chickens on ice for twenty years before they sell them, and they have to cut them with a hatchet, they are so hard. Is that true?" Thus asked Aunt Serena, who was famous for her cooking.

I did not ask any questions. I was ashamed of my relatives. Narrow-minded, provincial people. Then again, they were related to Martin just the same. One can't choose one's relatives, unfortunately.

Martin answered the chaotic questions calmly, occasionally hiding an amused smile, and then he talked about America in general. He said interesting things, most of them too good to be true, but his way of talking was absolutely assuring. So I learned, among other things, that during the war the miners wore silk shirts, drove their own automobiles, and ate meat for breakfast; and that anyone who was willing to work could support himself.

"It is an outrage!" chirped Aunt Fanny. "My son, who finished college a half a year ago, cannot find a position in any bank! Miners, common laborers, driving their own cars!"

Martin said in evident surprise:

"Why doesn't he look for some other kind of work?"

"What other kind of work?" asked Aunt Fanny. "He studied to be a banker. He does not know anything else."

Martin did not seem interested.

"But he can work if he is healthy and strong. Anybody knows how to be a busboy, brick carrier, factory hand."

Aunt Fanny gasped for air. Everybody was shocked. I was touched, too. God knows I disliked Aunt Fanny enough, but that was too much. Her son, the brother of a doctor, could not be a waiter!

My father turned to Martin, mildly expressing the general sentiment.

"But, Martin, a boy from our level cannot be a busboy, a brick carrier, or a common laborer. It is just impossible. It cannot be done."

Martin did not argue. But it was evident that he did not understand the reason for the general amazement.

They talked for a long time about America, and then later they were all eager to tell Martin of their own personal suffering throughout the war and revolution. I think he was bored, and I think he noticed me. He must have seen that I was different from the others, that I was bored with them, too; that I was his own kind.

I am going to America, I thought. *If miners, who are only common laborers, can have automobiles, silk shirts, and everything, what will happen if we, Charley and I, go there? We, with all our ability, intelligence and talent?*

The next day at lunch, I started to talk about Martin. I wanted to hear my father's opinion of him. He said, "Martin is a very important man. Clever, nice, rich, though a little bit strange."

I looked into space and played with my fork as I said, "Some day I shall be like him, too."

My father looked up and smiled a doubtful, belittling smile. He had his own idea about my future.

"What would you all say if I were to go to America, too?" I inquired coolly.

My older brother burst out laughing.

"You?" he cried. "To America? How silly!"

My father did not answer.

"It is not silly at all," I said. "I am going to America. It is decided."

"You are talking nonsense again," said my father. He didn't take me seriously at all.

"I mean every word I said," I announced with absolute determination. "It is decided."

My father's lips curled.

"I know those sudden and childish enthusiasms of yours. Keep quiet."

I was calm, as one sure of his point should be.

"Yes, I am enthusiastic," I said, "and I am going!"

My father looked at me a little severely and said, "Now, enough of this silliness!" He went on eating, as though he had settled the whole argument.

Slowly I reached into my pocket and took out my passport. I opened it. There was my picture with my signature, and the Italian visa.

"Here is my passport. I'm ready to go."

Everybody looked at me. There was fright in my mother's eyes. Father didn't say a word, but left the table. And I left the house for the afternoon.

That evening, dinner was eaten in awkward silence. After dinner my father asked me into his study.

"What is all this passport business?" he asked.

"I must have a passport to leave the country," I answered on the defensive.

"Do you want to be slapped again? Is that the idea?"

"You can slap me, father, but I am going to America."

"What do you mean, you are going? Who will give you the money for the fare? I won't give you a cent."

"I don't need your money. I have a passport to Trieste. I have money to go there. And from Italy I will work my way to America, just as Martin did. Charley is coming with me."

For a minute Father couldn't say a word because of the sudden rage that possessed him. Then he buried me under an avalanche of words.

"Very well, let's suppose you are going. Of course they need you there, for you are an excellent shoemaker, tailor, plumber, dentist. . . . What are you? Who are you? What is your trade? What do you know? What kind of work can you do to support yourself? But then you are going—President Wilson will meet you at the pier; the country's best orators will gather to meet you; young virgins, dressed in white, will throw flowers at your feet, and the best citizens will carry you on their shoulders into New York, which will be decorated with millions of flags and illuminated for the arrival of the freshest, laziest, and most conceited good-for-nothing in the world, the Champion Nobody! And now there has been enough of this idiocy! If you ever mention the word 'America' again in my decent house, I will give you the beating of your life!"

I did not say a word. My father left the room. But first he slapped my face twice. *Why always twice?* I wondered.

The next day I met Charley, as we had agreed, and we went to Teleky Square. Each of us carried a package. In mine there was a bed-sheet, a cigarette case, my watch, a broken table-lamp, and an inkwell. In Charley's package were several suits of clothes, shoes, a big military revolver in good condition, some small rugs, and a statuette. He took my package, too, as soon as we reached Teleky Square.

"Watch me get the money," he said confidently.

And he forced his way through the thick crowd, dragging me after him. He yelled and argued and bargained with the people who bought and sold secondhand things there. He seemed right at home. He seemed to know their languages, their peculiar slang. He was familiar with the psychology of this pandemonium. He praised them, scolded them, flattered them, cursed them, petted them, insulted them and was insulted, laughed and frowned, left the booths in pretended anger, and allowed them to drag him back.

In a couple of hours he had sold everything and obtained more money for various articles than we had hoped. We were about ready to leave this unrestricted madhouse of commerce, when he stopped abruptly in front of a booth and stared at an object there with narrowed eyes. Then he picked up the object of his admiration: an ugly pair of checkered trousers, slightly worn, and so loud they almost screeched.

"How much?" he asked, rubbing the material between two of his fingers with an expert's air. Then he added, pursing his lips, "Very bad material," and gave the man in the booth a suspicious look.

"Ten kronen," the man answered.

Charley laughed loudly. I didn't understand this at all, and I did not laugh with him. I pulled at his coat, and with signs and whispers I tried to express my bewilderment at his desire to buy the horrible trousers. But Charley ignored my signs completely.

"What? Ten kronen for this rag? You're crazy!" He began to laugh more loudly. I thought he had suddenly gone mad.

"All right, I'll let you have them for nine, but that is the lowest price. . . ."

"Four kronen," said Charley, coolly, and dropped the trousers as if he had lost interest in them. He took a few steps to go away.

The merchant was shocked. He pulled Charley back by the sleeve. They began to argue and quarrel. I was afraid the argument would end in blows. They insulted each other terribly. The merchant swore that seven kronen was the very lowest price, as he himself had paid more for them.

"All right," said Charley, "I'll give you the five kronen, but you must give me some other junk to boot." Pointing to a dirty, dilapidated, old samovar, he added, "Give me this dirty old thing."

The merchant yelled, "I said seven! . . . seven . . . seven!" Charley was about to walk away. The man still shouted, "Seven . . . seven . . . six . . ."

"Five . . ."

"Six . . . six . . . six . . ." and then, "five . . . five . . . take it!"

Charley took the trousers and the samovar and left the place.

I was boiling with anger.

"Charley, you are crazy! Buying that horrible pair of trousers!"

"You don't understand business, Paul," he said calmly, as he threw away the newspaper package containing the trousers.

"This samovar is worth at least a hundred and fifty kronen, but he didn't know it. The trousers were only the bait."

And Charley sold the samovar in an antique shop for a hundred kronen. We had acquired enough money to go to Trieste and to live for about a month. Teleky Square, the city's dirtiest, noisiest, cheapest marketplace, had given us the fare to Heaven—to America.

After dinner grandfather arrived at the house with Joseph. I suspected another family gathering—it seemed that there was always something to gather about in such a big family—and I wanted to sneak out of the house, but my mother kept me back with one sentence:

"Martin will be here also." I wanted to see Martin. I longed to talk to him, to tell him my plans.

Then the others came, Aunt Fanny and Uncle Hugo with his eyeglasses, and all the rest of them, but this time without children. "It must be a scandal," I thought. When my father noticed Aunt Fanny, he whispered to Mother, "Why did you ask Fanny to come? She would be delighted to put me to shame with her doctor son today. As if her son was the only doctor on earth. I will have one of my sons, or with God's help probably all three of them, become doctors."

"I am sorry, darling," mother whispered, "I didn't want to slight her."

Grandfather took his place at the head of the table in the most comfortable armchair. Joseph sat on his left, and my father on his right. Martin was there, too. Grandfather looked around sharply to see whether every grown member of the family was present, and then he started to talk.

"My children," he began, "I want to tell you why we have come together tonight. Bertha's son, Paul, wants to go to America. We are here to decide how we can prevent this."

My heart stopped beating, and my face turned red. I was shocked beyond words. Everyone looked at me reproachfully. Some of them smiled sarcastically. What did they want of me? Where did all these strange people get the nerve to interfere in my life? Who were they to me? I was humiliated. A gathering of butchers, fat bankers, spectacled merchants, Uncle Hugos and Aunt Fannys, were about to decide my fate, my life! Outrageous! As I looked over this hostile, malicious circle, my eyes rested for a moment on a pair of dark, lively eyes that seemed to be smiling at me. Martin's eyes.

I was about to jump up, to denounce all of them, when Uncle Hugo began to talk.

"Well," he said, "I really don't know what to say. . . ." (*Then why say it?*) "I was suspicious of Paul long before I heard of this horrible thing. I have often caught him going to cafés—at his age! He might even be playing billiards!" (*I've never heard that billiards is one of the seven deadly sins.*) "Who knows?" *I am going to learn to play billiards!*)

Then he stood up and looked at me, pointing an accusing finger while his voice rose to the highest pitch of condemnation:

"Do you know that I was thirty-three years of age when I went to the café for the first time in my life?"

Uncle Hugo looked around complacently to collect the admiration he expected in all eyes. Then he went on.

"Personally, I think Paul is lost. If he has such thoughts already, he is no good, no matter what we might do for him." (*I must become a champion billiard player!*)

My father's face was grim.

Aunt Fanny sighed so deeply that her enormous bosom expanded above the table, and said smugly, "Thank God I have no such troubles with my sons. One of them is a doctor, and the other will be a bank director."

My mother's eyes were full of tears. I felt that my parents were ashamed of me. Every one had something to say.

"Decent children should not leave the house without permission." (*I'm going to stand up in a minute and tell them what I think.*) "One should not leave one's country under any circumstances." (*My narrow-minded relatives! I'll tell them!*) "I think we should do everything in our power to save Bertha's son from utter ruination." (*I am proud that I do not belong here, and I would be very much ashamed if you should find any reason to be proud of me.*) "Paul will be grateful to us later when he has become a decent, honored, and respected citizen, that we prevented him from disgracing his family." (*My life is my own and I shall do with it what I please. I did not choose to be your relative, and I won't allow you to take advantage of the circumstance.*)

"Paul has no reason to leave this country. Only criminals and ruined peasants are migrating to America." (*Relatives are good for one thing: to interfere with one's freedom!*) "It is the sacred duty of the whole family to stand together as one man." (*I resent your treating me as if I were a criminal or a child. I am the master of my fate. I want you to know that no one can keep me back if I want to go—and I am going!*) "It is a catastrophe. . . ."

Grandfather now interrupted the endless, and useless:

"I think we should consult our beloved son, Martin, who has just come back from America, adding new honor and esteem to the family name with his success. The sensible thing to do is to let him decide in this unfortunate affair."

I looked at Martin. His eyes still smiled. I trembled, and was ready to hate him, too.

Everybody looked at him expectantly. And he said, in a very matter-of-fact way:

"Why are you talking so much about it? Let him go, if he wants to. If he doesn't like it, he will come back."

Dead silence. Everybody was shocked. Martin had spoiled their self-important posturing. Uncle Hugo almost choked on a piece of cake. Joseph looked at grandfather and waited for the final sentence. Grandfather seemed to understand the meaning of Martins words. Looking at Martin, he said quietly:

"There is something in that. Perhaps we should let him go."

My father looked at Martin, astonished and bewildered. I wanted to run to him, hug him, and kiss his hand. Such a grand uncle. He did not wait for the conference to break up, but took his hat and started to leave. Before he left the room, he turned to me and said, "Paul, do you want to come to the café with me?"

I made half a motion to run, but my father checked me.

"You are going to stay here," he said. "Sit down."

But I went out to the other room with Martin, stammering confused thanks.

"Don't worry," Martin said, "Ten years ago they held just such a conference about my going. You have no passport and no money, I understand. I could give you money, but I don't want to. Anybody can go there with money. You must reach America by your own strength. America is not a good country for weaklings. If you can get there without anybody's help, you'll be successful. Here is my business card. I am leaving tomorrow. Look me up in New York. Good luck!"

I went back to the dining room, a victorious man, in the midst of a mournful and beaten gathering. Before I could prevent it, Aunt Fanny hugged and kissed me, with tears in her eyes, sighing, "Poor Bertha. . . ." Then she turned to my mother.

"I don't know how you make that nutcake, Bertha. It's simply delicious. May I take some home to my doctor son?"

Slowly all the guests departed. I kissed my grandfather's hand. He gave me some good advice, all of which was to be found in the Bible, too.

When we were left alone, my father said to my mother, in a trembling voice, "Have his baggage ready." Then, more hopefully, "He'll be back from Ujpest anyway."

Ujpest is the first stop the train makes after leaving Budapest.

CHAPTER 4

THE DAY BEFORE I left, I decided to go to the Zoo to see Klari and say goodbye to her. I sent her a letter by messenger, which read:

> *Klari darling, I must see you once more. I am going to America. I want to say goodbye to you before I go. Please write your answer and give it to this boy, who will deliver it to me.*
> *Paul*

Klari did not write an answer, but she came to the corner with the boy. I cannot describe my emotion when I saw her. She was so beautiful, so lovely, as she came toward me, smiling sweetly. She offered me her hand, which I shook.

"What is the trouble, Paul?" she said. "Why are you so excited? You need not write falsehoods to me if you want to see me."

"Falsehoods? What do you mean."

"About America," she answered. "Why are you lying to me?"

Without a word I produced my passport form my pocket.

"Here, darling," I said, "is my passport, and tomorrow morning at eleven o'clock, I am going to Vienna. From there

I am going to Trieste, and the next stop will be America. I am not lying."

Silence. Then she turned to me.

"Come with me, Paul," she said.

I went with her happily behind the soft drink stand, where we had spent so many beautiful hours together. She looked sad, and we could not say much to each other for a long time.

"Klari, darling," I said, "I feel that I am a grown man now, going to unknown, faraway places. I will come back with money, and everything, and then . . ."

It was hard to speak sure, clean-cut sentences while fighting back the tears. But she understood.

"Yes, dear, when you have money you will send for me, or come for me, and I will go with you."

I could hardly speak. I had thought that I would tell her very nice and clever things, but all the time I had but one thought in my mind. I wanted to kiss her, somehow, but I could not find the necessary gesture.

The time came when I had to go home. We came out of our hiding place and stood in front of the stand. People were walking up and down. It was impossible to kiss her.

"Goodbye, Klari. . . ."

She did not say a word, but with a sudden, marvelous gesture she hugged me and kissed me in front of her mother. She was the most wonderful girl that ever lived. Oh, I was ready to die for her, to do anything for her. . . .

In the morning the whole house was upset. Everybody tried to help me pack my belongings. At breakfast there was an argument, for mother had got up very early and had cooked and baked things, partly for an early lunch and partly for me to take along on the trip. Father opposed this very much. In a few hours I would be in Vienna, he said, and it would be childish to give me roast chicken and apple strudel; it would be provincial and old-fashioned. Mother cried softly, and no matter how my father tried to soothe her, she just continued to cry. After breakfast my father called me into his study. I found him walking up and down. He was visibly embarrassed. With great effort he started to speak.

"Now listen, Paul, there are things . . . in life . . . I wanted to talk to you about. Now that you are leaving the paternal home . . . a grown man . . ." He started to cough. "You are going out into life . . . with its many dangers and pitfalls for the inexperienced and young. It is my duty to warn you . . . no matter how embarrassing it is for both of us . . . We are men . . . grown-up men . . . and we should talk frankly. There are things about women that you ought to know, for there will be nobody to tell you. . . ."

For a minute I looked at my father. I was embarrassed also. What should I answer? Should I tell him that I had read all the books printed about sex? That I was familiar with the literature pertaining to sex? That I had read Zola, Hans Heinz Ewers, Schnitzler, Boccaccio, and Casanova? Should I give him a lecture on Kraft-Ebing, Weininger, Freud, and Bolsche? I looked at him: lovely, naïve father of mine, with a dear tremble in his voice, fighting back his tears. I felt a lump in my throat. I let him finish his speech without saying a word. Finally his voice broke, and a sad, heartrending, choking sound burst forth—that terrible sound with which only strong men can cry, perhaps once in a lifetime. He quickly left the room, and I stood there before his desk where I had stood so many times before and been slapped. I felt that I should have told him to slap me now, hard, in the face, twice.

My mother called me to come out to the kitchen. She sent the servant out, and we were alone. My mother was crying.

"Paul, please hide this package. It is some cake and roast chicken . . . the leg . . . I know you like it so much. They don't understand. Don't show it to anybody. And here is some money . . . not much. Nobody knows about it."

She kissed me, and wiped her tears with her apron. Dear, dear mother, like those mothers in the fairy stories who baked cakes with their tears for their adventurous sons to take on long journeys, and with the cake, a piece of their mother's heart.

I never knew it would be so hard to go. For a moment I wished that the whole thing had not happened. But I had to go. America was calling me.

About eleven o'clock Charley's parents came down, and the two families went to the pier in two cabs. My parents, big brother, sister, little brother, all came to the pier. We talked very little in the cab. My father gave me some general advice—to take care of my hands so that they should not get chapped by the wind, to be careful about food, not to be friendly with strangers, and so on. General kissing and crying, and then we boarded the ship.

"Look who is there, Paul," Charley exclaimed.

"Where?"

"Not far from your mother, on the right."

I looked. I saw a girl, a darling, sweet young girl timidly waving a handkerchief, with a sad smile on her lips. Klari, my darling Klari. I waved back to her.

My mother looked, and slowly she started to go toward her. I shivered with excitement. What would happen? Klari started to go away, but my mother reached out her hand, and with a slow gesture, put her arm around her, and gently drew her into the family group. My father looked at her also, looked at them, tenderly: two women, two weeping women, weeping for his son.

I wanted to jump off the ship. *Good God, why was I going to America if Klari, and my father, and my mother, there . . . together.* . . . But the boat started. The ship went faster and faster. The waving handkerchiefs became smaller and smaller . . . like earthbound little white birds, fluttering. And then I did not see them anymore. I held Charley's hand, and we looked toward the pier, toward that brown, formless spot. . . . There were people . . . my people . . . and here was I, leaving them, leaving Budapest . . . Hungary . . . and then Europe. What was I going to do in America? Why was I going there? Was I a shoemaker? Was I a carpenter? No, I was a nobody, and I was going to starve there. I was frightened. Yet it would be shameful to turn back. No! No! I was not a coward. I was going on!

When we reached Vienna my depression disappeared. A beautiful city, lovely people, and freedom, blessed, yearned-for-freedom, such as I had never experienced before. Nobody to answer to for anything. I could go home as late as I pleased.

We went to a café, and to prove to myself that I was free, I started to play billiards for the first time in my life. It was boring, very boring. Even the thought of Uncle Hugo was not enough inducement to keep it up. Then we walked about the streets. I was sleepy, I longed for bed, though it wasn't later than eleven o'clock. I tried to cheer myself with the thought of my freedom, but I was tired, and on the first day of my freedom I went to bed about eleven-thirty.

CHAPTER 5

WE STAYED IN Vienna three days. Charley had to visit relatives, to attend to some business matter for his father, and to look up a woman who had been governess at their house some years before, and with whom Charley said he had had a love affair.

Under different circumstances, Vienna would have been a great thrill to me, for I had never been alone in a city as marvelous as this one. But though it was famous for its colorful nightlife, and though I longed to see this nightlife, I did not feel at ease there. I was restless. What did I care about Vienna, when I wanted to go to America? For me, Vienna was only a way station. Charley, on the other hand, was anxious to stay longer. But I objected to such an unnecessary and expensive delay. We were on our way to America.

So we went to Trieste. The city frightened me a little, though it was not as big as Vienna. It was a foreign city, and we did not speak the language of the natives. In Vienna we had felt more at home, for we understood German. But here everybody talked Italian or Slavish. I encouraged myself by repeating that this was but another station, soon to be left behind. The very first day we found out that only union workers were employed on the steamers, and at that time there were thirty thousand experienced sailors unemployed.

It was a terrible blow to me. The whole thing had looked so simple.

"Well," Charley said, "we can go home." And he sighed. I was shocked.

"You are a coward," I said angrily. "Turning back the very first day, at the very first difficulty! You may go, if you want, but I am staying."

We had a quarrel. I was not going to turn back or, at least, not so soon. Give all of Budapest something to laugh at? Never! And what would Klari say? She would hate me! And my father—he would mock me for the rest of my life. Charley insisted that my father would have no reason to laugh at me, for I would at least come back from Trieste, and not from Ujpest, as he had predicted. But it was useless. I was not going to turn back.

The next few days we were utterly despondent. I hardly said a word, but Charley kept talking about America. All the bad and frightening things he had ever read or heard he now related over and over again, exaggerating and coloring incidents here and there. I am afraid that half the horrors he told me about America were born in his vivid and ready imagination. But America was the same wonderful dream to me, and the difficulties in the way made it seem all the more desirable.

One afternoon Charley came home to our cheap furnished room, in a great excitement.

"Do you know who I met today?" he asked breathlessly.

"No."

"Tolnay. He is the president of the biggest steamship company on earth. He knows my people and was very friendly to me. He told me about a new order, a government order, under which, from now on, no more ships can go to America. No more ships! Do you understand what that means? It is hopeless to stay here anymore. Absolutely hopeless. If we stay we will starve to death. We have very little money left, just enough for a few weeks more, and then . . . death! We must go back."

I knew the whole thing was impossible.

"What government gave that order?" I inquired.

"My God! The government! What do you mean 'what government?' It is a government order. No more ships."

"Impossible! Nobody and no government gave such an order. I am afraid that you did not meet Tolnay."

He did not say a word for a moment, and then he confessed.

"No, Paul," he said, "I didn't. We have enough money to go back and we ought not wait until our last pennies are gone. We should go now."

"I am not going back. I would rather die than go back. I must go to America. My father would laugh at me."

"Now listen, Paul, be sensible. Vienna is the city. Vienna is the place we should live. We can speak German. We will do things there, we will be somebodies in Vienna, and we will be near Budapest if anything unexpected happens. America was not made for us. Strange people. We do not understand the language. We have no trade. America is for Americans only. After all, every place is alike. There must be streets there, just as there are streets here or in Vienna . . . streets and apartment houses . . . and rooms. Uninteresting, boring. Why go so far away from Budapest? We can be our own bosses in Vienna, too. I have relatives there. Please, Paul, come back with me. I have decided to go. I am going back to

Vienna, beautiful, friendly, darling Vienna. It was stupid of us to leave it. But it is not too late. Come with me."

I was touched. It would have been nice to go home. Vienna was near Budapest. Klari was near Vienna. But I could not have my father laugh at me. I was ashamed even to think of seeing him after an unsuccessful attempt. I had to wait. Something would happen. The situation could not be so bad; there could not be no hope.

"No, Charley, I am going to stay here. I don't want you to go back, either, but if you are going, I will stay alone."

Charley hugged me.

"You will come with me. Can't you see how stubborn you are? It is impossible to stay. You will starve in this stupid Trieste so far away from home."

The argument ended with the decision that Charley would go to Vienna, and I would stay in Trieste. It was so bad to be left alone that I even forgot to hate him for his cowardice.

Charley decided to go immediately. We went to the railway station and found that there was a train for Vienna that night. We walked up and down in front of the station. We had one hour yet. Charley still tried to convince me. I was fighting with myself. I had to show Klari that I could do big things, and could not have my father laugh at me.

Charley pleaded with me:

"Even now you have time. Come with me, Paul, come!"

"No, I am going to stay here."

"All right. I will give you my shaving set. I will get another in Vienna. And your trousers are torn. Here. Mine will be a little bit too long for you, but they are a good pair of trousers, and it will be easy to have them mended. And here . . . some money. It will be enough for you for a few days. We will write to each other, and if you need anything, I will send it."

"You are very nice, Charley, and it is terrible to part with you, but I cannot go back. If I get to America, I shall send you money and an affidavit from there, and then you can join me, and we will be together again."

Charley smiled.

"No," he answered, "I am through with the America idea forever. We'll see each other in Budapest."

The train pulled in. Charley was trembling with happiness. I was trembling with fright.

"I'll see you in Budapest next week," he said, and laughed.

"You will not," I answered, tears in my voice. The train started. He kept calling my name in a sincerely affectionate voice, calling me, urging me to jump aboard. The train disappeared, and I was left alone.

I stayed at the station a long time, why, I did not know. No, I did not want to wait for the next train. I only asked the man about it, for no reason whatsoever. I just wanted to know. The next train to Vienna was in the morning. No, I was not going.

The station was deserted, and I left it. too, with very slow steps and a heavy heart. Then I braced up, started to whistle, and went into a dingy little restaurant to eat my dinner.

As I opened the door, I stopped abruptly, for I heard a Hungarian song, my favorite Hungarian song. A young man was standing in the center of the room, in a cloud of heavy smoke, and he was singing the song in a warm, pleasant Hungarian voice. *He must be a Hungarian,* I thought, *a newcomer at that, for otherwise he would sing Italian.* For a moment I listened, and when he started to sing the sad refrain, I stepped up to him, put my hand on his shoulder, and joined in. He looked at me in surprise, then understood the situation, and we continued singing together. I had not thought before I did this. I was sad, and it was a Hungarian song, and the young man seemed sympathetic, so I just had to sing with him. It was a very clever move, as I found out in a few minutes. When the singing was over, my strange Hungarian friend went to the people in the restaurant, holding his hat in his hands, and almost everybody gave him some money. It was not much—centissimi only—but real money.

He came back to me, winked, and we left the place together. Outside he counted the money carefully, and without saying a word he gave me half of all he had collected. I was astonished.

"What do you mean?" I asked him.

"Well, you can count it over if you want to. I gave you exactly half of what I got. What's wrong with that?"

"My God, I didn't mean to do it for money. Here, take it back. It is yours."

"No, you earned it. Do you know that I got more than twice as much as I usually get? They like two people better than one, and everybody gives more money that way. They think two need more than one. They are right."

"What is your name?" I asked.

"Bandi Vida."

"Where do you live?"

"I am just looking for a place to live. I am an actor from Budapest. I want to go to America somehow. I have been here for two months. This is a tough city, this Trieste."

"Well," I answered, "My friend just left me, and I need a roommate. Would you come with me? I want to go to America, too."

"Great! We can get by more easily together. We can work this way until something happens, and then we can go to America together."

CHAPTER 6

BANDI MOVED INTO my room, brining his belongings: some linens and a few books. It was very pleasant to live with him. We continued to sing in restaurants, though I was not much of a singer. We even learned a few Italian songs. But business was bad. Often we went home with only a few centissimi as our evening's earnings. The money I had brought from home was gone, and Bandi had none, either. But somehow I was slow to realize that poverty had overtaken us. I could not imagine that some day I might have no breakfast, lunch, or dinner, and perhaps no place to sleep. I had heard of such things, but it was so much fiction to me, for I had never personally known anyone to whom they had happened.

The first day I had to do without lunch was frightening. I felt like going back to Budapest, but luckily I had no money for the fare. Our rent was not paid, and we had no money. Hunger wasn't as bad as I thought it would be, physically, but it certainly dampened our spirits. We stayed in our room for several days, waiting for something, neither of us knew exactly what.

One day the landlady became suspicious because we did not go out to eat, and asked questions. We explained that in Hungary things were quite different from Italy. People in our country usually had no regular times for meals—they ate at all odd hours.

It seemed that she had her own opinion of Hungary, for after that she came to our room quite often, bringing delicious potatoes she had just cooked for us to taste. We tasted the whole dish away in no time. We managed the food problem by getting stale bread in bakeries, sometimes for nothing, sometimes for very little money, and what with all the water we could have right at home, we existed. But I could not sleep. The words "poverty, "hunger," and "starvation" hammered in my head at night. I did not mention this to Bandi. I was small, I looked like a child, and so I had to act more bravely than a grown-up person, to make people believe that I was a man, ready to face life gamely.

We kept up the singing, but the income was meager. Sometimes nothing but a few cigarettes. This was really a blessing, for hunger for tobacco was worse than hunger for food.

Finally the landlady told us that although it broke her heart, we would have to move if we did not pay the rent by the next morning. Bandi behaved suspiciously that day. He did not talk much, and I was afraid that he had lost his courage. Probably he was thinking of going back to Budapest, I thought. That evening, when we came home from the café, where we had sung without any financial success, Bandi, after a long and heavy silence, said, "Listen, Paul, you can do me a big favor. Go to the park and take a walk . . . just for a half hour. Then you can come back. Please don't ask any questions. You'll know everything when you return."

I looked at him and agreed. I went to the park and walked. I was alone, and sad. What could be the reason of Bandi's changed attitude toward me? Then suddenly it flashed through my mind that perhaps he was going to move, or leave the city and go back to Budapest, in the half hour. The ungrateful wretch! So, everybody was leaving me! The thought hurt me terribly. It was an actual physical pain—not in my heart, but somewhere in my chest, between the ribs, or in my stomach. I could hardly stand the pain, but I did not want to go away. He could go—to hell!

The half hour elapsed and I went home with my heart throbbing in my throat. I tiptoed to the door and listened. Not a sound. He must have gone away. The dirty coward! I opened the door and was afraid I had opened the wrong one. The whole room was decorated with colored paper. But it was our room. I was flabbergasted. Bandi wasn't in sight. I looked around. One the table was a package in red paper, with a big sign on it!

"For Paul. Happy Birthday."

My God! It was my birthday! I had forgotten. I opened the package with trembling hands. A box—what could it be? I opened it, and tears began to run down my face.

"Bandi!"

He stepped out from behind the curtain with a shy smile on his lips, and I rushed to him and hugged him and cried and cried, for in the box there was tobacco . . . lovely, yellow tobacco, and a package of cigarette paper. We both cried. Soon I started to smoke. Bandi watched me, but no matter how I begged him, he would not smoke. He told me later that he collected the cigarette butts facetiously dropped in his hat by humorous gentlemen in the cafés, with the idea of saving the tobacco for my birthday.

Finally I forced him to light a cigarette. I rolled one for him and we sat, and smoked, inhaling the lovely smoke, deep,

deep to our very hearts, to our very souls, to warm ourselves with it. I told him of my terrible thoughts of him, and he wasn't even angry. A friend!

Next day we moved. That is, we left our room. We had to leave all our belongings there for the rent we owed. We went to the waterfront. A steamer had arrived from America. We earned a little money by helping the passengers with their baggage—enough for bread and cigarettes. We slept in a park. Then I sold my hat for a lire, and we ate the next day. It rained all day long and I had no hat. Bandi forced me to accept his hat, and the rest of the day we wore it alternately, changing its ownership every half hour. Bandi recited Hungarian poetry—intoxicating, feverish poems—to make us forget and feel better.

In the evening we went to a very cheap, low dive, notorious for its suspicious clientele, to sing and try to make some money. A group of ship's officers came into the place. They were obviously slumming. We noticed that they were Hungarians, from different ships. I winked significantly at Bandi: ship's officers, Hungarians, probably from ships that went to America. I was excited. Bandi understood my signal. Slowly, but unostentatiously, with perfect teamwork, we turned toward the officers and started to sing. We sang the finest Hungarian songs. The thought came to my mind that we were working as two cheap little cabaret singers, smiling and singing for the suckers, and I was a bit ashamed of myself. Bandi was smiling toward them, and they soon invited us to their table and paid for our dinner. One of them, a gigantic man who went by the name of Peaches, was the one I had my eye on. I had a hunch that I could work him successfully. So as we ate I talked to him, racking my brains for the wittiest and smartest topics. I made the giant laugh many times, and Bandi looked at me with an appreciative eye.

As we were talking, a scene caught my eye. A couple was sitting at a far table: a middle-aged man, and a woman made up to appear young and attractive. He voice was affected. She was busily making signs above the head of her companion to a handsome Italian. She made a date with him shamelessly, not caring whether her companion noticed or not. She raised her hand, sparkling with cheap jewelry, and held up two fingers to the other man. It must have meant two o'clock.

"I bet there will be a pretty fight if the other man notices that his lady love is making a date before his very eyes."

Peaches turned toward them and watched. The man with the girl turned and leaned nearer to her. The girl threw her arms around him, and at the same time laughed and winked at the other man. Suddenly Peaches hissed between his teeth.

"Damn that girl!" he said. "That man is blind."

And then I saw it, too. The blind man was turning his head around helplessly, as if sensing that something was wrong.

"You must pick a fight with the other man," said Peaches. I laughed. It was a good joke. I, a small and not too strong young man, should pick a fight with a husky young Italian? I stopped laughing when Peaches's expression showed that he meant what he said. I? A peaceful and harmless person? But I remembered that I wanted to go to America, and Peaches was a marine officer. Then Peaches said to me:

"Just go there and give him a knock. If he says something, tell him this one word." He told me an Italian word, which

I repeated, though I had no idea what it meant. "Don't be afraid," he added, "I'll be there in time."

I got up. I was shivering a little. Well, I was ready for the beating of my life, but I couldn't risk losing the friendship of Peaches. I could live but once. I didn't care.

I passed by and stepped on the Italian's foot. Just a little, almost accidentally, really. He yelled something at me. I didn't know what it was, so I did not feel insulted. Then I opened my mouth, and against my better judgment I spoke the Italian word. Not angrily, for I wasn't angry. And I am sure that my pronunciation lacked the spirit behind the meaning of the word. But I said it loudly. The Italian jumped up and grabbed my arm, shouting something in Italian. At this moment Peaches came over to us, big and threatening. They said a few words to each other in Italian, and then they started to fight. Peaches fought enthusiastically, joyously, laughingly. He took blows as though he were made of stone. They did not even shake him. He spared his opponent to make the fight last longer. He played with him, laughing and teasing like Cyrano de Bergerac in his famous duel.

"All right, old man, finish it. Let's go!" one of the officers called out. Peaches knocked the man out with a single blow, and we left the place together. We went to their hotel and stayed there for several hours. Before we left, I was a great friend of Peaches. He gave me plenty of cigarettes and asked for my address. I told him frankly that we were going to move in the morning, and I didn't know where to. He asked me to look him up on the ship—which was scheduled to sail for America soon.

We had no place to sleep, but we couldn't have slept in the best bed in the world. We were too excited. We walked and talked about America.

Peaches was a kind-hearted brute, but still a brute, and he loved to fight. Once we were sitting in a café again, and I was dreaming aloud about America, when I noticed that Peaches was not in a good mood.

"Shall I pick a fight?" I asked timidly, secretly hoping that he was not in a fighting mood. He wanted to fight, and I got up and looked around the place. I picked out a tall, strong-looking man, and skillfully started to get into trouble with him. Peaches had told me words that would insult every Italian, and this time they were successful. As usual Peaches interrupted our fight, and won, of course. It always happened that way. When we left the place, Peaches was preoccupied, and apparently heard nothing of what I was saying. He was busy with his own thoughts. Now and then he said to himself: "Impossible. . . . It can't be done."

"What can't be done?" I asked.

"No," he continued, still oblivious to my presence. "Nonsense, nobody could go to America that way."

"Which way? What do you mean?" My heart was in my throat.

"No . . . forget it. I was just thinking out loud, but I see it is impossible. You would die before the ship would reach America."

I thought desperately for some convincing phrase, for I knew that everything depended on my words.

"Peaches," I said, earnestly, "you do not know the situation. I can do almost anything. If it were possible to be tied to the ship and swim after her, I would be willing to do it. I can go through anything. Once I did not eat for six days, just for fun, and I did not even feel it. I can go without sleep for any length of time. I can work harder than any strong man. I have a way of hypnotizing myself, and when I am in that condition, I can make myself do anything. I don't know just what you mean, but whatever it is, I can do it. I am sure. People do not die so easily. Please tell me what way you are talking about."

Peaches looked blankly into space, and after a long pause, said:

"I was thinking of hiding you on the boat—in the hold. But it is too difficult. I don't think you could stand it."

"Please, Peaches, try to understand. Nothing is impossible. America is the prize. I am ready to do anything and everything."

After a long, long conversation in which I tried to convince him that he could not think of anything that I was not willing to do, finally he said:

"All right. If you want to come as much as you say, I don't care. You can come with us to America. The boat will be ready to leave in a few days. I will hide you, and you will see what will happen. I am willing to do what I can."

I was so happy that for a minute I could not believe he meant what he said.

"Peaches," I cried, "do you really mean it? Can I tell Bandi? Can we depend on your promise? It would be terrible to be disappointed."

Peaches turned to me, red with anger:

"Where do you get that 'we' stuff? I was not talking about anybody else but you. You can come along, but nobody else. What do you think? Do you think I want to take all Budapest to America? You are crazy!"

It was awful. He had just given me hope, and then took it away immediately. I would rather have died than have gone without Bandi. It would have been a dirty thing to do. I could not even think about it. I would find some other way. I was sure. We must!

At that time we lived in the Bosquetto, a little parklike forest on the outskirts of the city. It was nice to live there, free and happy, with no worrying about the rent. We got up very early in the morning, and before people were about, we went to strange backyards and shaved and washed ourselves at strange wells. It seldom happened that the owner of the house caught us shaving and chased us away, but when such a thing happened, we went to somebody else's backyard and finished the job there. There were many backyards in Trieste.

That evening, when I met Bandi, I was in a very bad mood, and Bandi did not know what had happened to me.

"I just hate that Peaches person." I said bitterly to Bandi.

"Has anything happened between you?" Bandi asked me.

"No, not a thing," I assured him. And that was the truth. Not a thing.

The next morning we awoke early, and having shaved and washed ourselves, we were lucky enough to get some very good and not very stale bread from the bakery. We ate the bread happily on the street, even though our situation at the moment was not very good. The future seemed promising, and somehow, in spite of everything, life was sweet and we were full of hope. After a few hours of window-shopping, we went to the railroad station. We had no particular reason to go there, but there is something exciting, something alluring about railroad stations. The smoke, the yelling, the hurrying, strange people kissing each other goodbye, happy reunions, little comedies and little tragedies.

We had no money to go anywhere, but at the station we felt important, perhaps because others might think that we were going somewhere to do something important.

As we walked up and down, Bandi looked down at the ground suddenly, picked up something, I could not see what, and after a moment, he whispered to me in a strained and excited voice, “Let’s go.”

I did not know what he was nervous about, but I followed him, and for a long time we just walked next to each other in silence. Finally he turned to me, looked around carefully, and when he saw that there was nobody around, he broke out:

“I found fifty lire.”

I thought he was joking, because a long time ago I had decided that there were no witches, no devils, no ghosts, and not a fifty lire bill on earth.

He saw the doubt on my face, so he produced the magic paper from his pocket, and showed it to me.

It was a fifty lire banknote, a little bit dirty, but otherwise one might have taken it for a new bill. Fifty lire! Wealth . . . happiness . . . life . . . everything . . . dinner . . . breakfast . . . more dinner . . . a room to live in . . . a private place to wash . . . Fifty lire! Impossible!

Bandi collected his wits first. We went out to our living quarters in the Bosquetto, sat down on the grass, and started to talk about the money. What would we do with it? Of course we would eat. The most delicious dinner on earth would not cost more than one lire. If we had wanted to save, we could have had one for fifty centesimi.

We talked for hours, but could not decide about anything definite. As we went back toward the city, Bandi stopped suddenly in the middle of the conversation. He was staring at something in a store window, and in a moment he disappeared behind the door. My heart beat heavily as I stood there waiting for him. Finally he came out with a big package in his hand. I was afraid to ask him what it was.

He bought several things, but everything was packed in mysterious packages. We stopped in front of a house, on the Piazza Pozzo del Mare, very near the place where we had lived before. We rented a beautiful furnished room for five lire a week, and Bandi paid the rent two weeks in advance.

We moved into our new place immediately, carefully locked the doors, and opened our packages. The first thing I saw was a large bottle of perfume. Later on I found that Bandi had paid thirteen lire for it. It was lovely perfume, but we did not use any of it. However, I understood his reason for buying it immediately, for I remembered how many times I had noticed the same bottle of perfume in the window. Somehow that beautiful bottle with the colored ribbons was the symbol of wealth and happiness, and considering the lovely fragrance and the size of the bottle, he had not paid too much for it.

He also bought a giant bar of chocolate, enough for both of us for at least a week; he bought cigarettes for ten lire, and many other small things.

We had some money left, too. The next day we did not want to go out of the room. It was a bright, sunny day, but we decided to stay in all day. After spending so much time at the Bosquetto, we did not want to see open spaces for a while. The next day we went up to our former landlady to give her some money and take away our belongings. She told us that

Peaches had come there looking for me several times in the last few days. Bandi was curious.

"He is not good," I said. "He is nothing but a bluffer and a liar. We should not waste time talking about him."

"You had better go to the ship and find out what he wants from you," said Bandi.

I could not find him on the ship, but I left my new address for him.

That evening when we came home I found a note on the table, which read, "Be at the coffee house tonight at ten. Peaches."

I knew it was no use arguing with him, he was a stubborn man, but I went to the coffee house anyway.

"The ship is leaving tomorrow," he told me. "This is the last day. Have you changed your mind? Do you want to come alone, or do you prefer to stay here?"

"I am not going without Bandi," I answered stubbornly. I was furious. I was sure he could stow us both. I might stay in Italy forever and have Italian children, who would address me in Italian with a Trieste dialect. I might grow a long beard and marry an Italian girl. I might never get closer to America than to read about it in books. But I was not going alone. That was all there was to it.

Peaches was not in a cheerful mood, either.

"Make up your mind, stupid, and be quick about it," he said. "This may be your only chance."

I could not stand it any longer. I jumped up from the table and shouted, "You can go to hell or to America, but I am going to stay with Bandi."

I could not control myself. All my hopes had vanished. I had to do something. I felt like murdering everybody.

Fortunately my eyes fell on a peaceful but husky Italian who stood near to our table. I was red. I jumped on him, and before he could realize what it was all about, I was hitting him with my all my might, angrily shouting that Italian word. I fought like a tiger, a rather puny tiger, to be exact. But the Italian was strong and tore himself away from me—or, rather, tore me off himself. By that time Peaches took charge of the situation, though this time I had not picked the fight to please him. He was angry, too. He hit the man with whom I was fighting, and before the poor fellow had a chance to get up, Peaches started to fight with somebody else. He fought with two men at the same time, and after a hard struggle he won.

He winked at me, and we left the place together.

Peaches evidently felt much better after the fight, for he said:

"For the last time I am asking you: do you want to come with me alone to America, or not?"

"For the last time and forever—no!" I shouted.

"All right, then, I will take you both. You are lucky. I had decided to take you only if you stuck to Bandi. If you had agreed to come alone, I would not have taken either of you. You are a great boy, Paul."

"Peaches, do you really mean it?" I managed to say.

"Of course I do."

"Can I go home and tell Bandi?"

"Yes. And I will see you tonight, after dinner."

I did not even thank him. I ran. I wanted to fly. To be quicker I jumped on a streetcar. It moved so slowly I could not wait. I jumped off and started to run. I noticed that the streetcar passed me, but I did not care. Somehow it seemed faster to run.

I flew up the stairs and yelled, "Bandi! Bandi! We are going to America! The boat leaves tomorrow! Tomorrow will be the most glorious tomorrow of all days!"

"What do you mean? Tell me? What is all this?"

"It's Peaches! Tomorrow! The ship—his ship . . . our ship starts tomorrow! And we are going! It is all settled. He is going to hide us on the ship. He will be here tonight."

Bandi was crying. We hugged each other; we danced around the room. It was real happiness. We were the two happiest men in Trieste. That night Peaches came. We bought colored papers and small flags, and when he entered the room, it was decorated in his honor.

"We start at eight o'clock tomorrow morning," he said. "You will come with me tonight, and I'll get you a place to sleep for the night. From here the boat goes to Venice. There we take on cargo. You don't have to hide from here to Venice. I shall tell the captain that my friends are going to Venice to visit some relatives. In Venice you will leave the boat. When the time comes for you to return I'll let you know. From Venice, we go to America. I'll hide both of you. You'll see the rest."

Bandi was breathless. He went to Peaches and shook his hand.

"I don't know how to thank you, but . . ."

Peaches interrupted him.

"Don't be foolish. I did nothing. But," he pointed to me, "you have a very good friend in Paul. I told him I would take him, alone. He would not go. He did not want to go without you. You can depend on him, Bandi. He drew a deep breath, but his voice failed him. All he could say was, "Paul!"

We started to pack our things.

"You really don't know what you are doing for us," I said to Peaches. "We would have given our lives for a chance to go. And now these lives are yours."

We boarded the ship that night without any difficulty, and in the morning, after a sleepless night, we sailed—for America! Yes. Venice first, but then—America!

After a short and pleasant trip we arrived at Venice. There we thanked the captain for his kindness and said goodbye to everybody. Peaches came ashore with us as we left the ship.

CHAPTER 7

We were in Venice, the rendezvous of the world's lovers, for whom handsome young gondoliers created a romantic atmosphere with a perpetual repetition of *Santa Lucia*. We were in Venice, not far from the famous pigeons of St. Mark's Place; Venice, the city of beautiful paintings, ancient buildings, beautiful buildings, and ancient paintings—and we did not care to look at any of it.

For us, Venice was merely a station on the way to America; it was not a city in itself.

We spent most of our time there on the docks, close to our ship, the most important ship that ever sailed the seas. We hardly slept from the excitement, and the anxiety of watching our ship for fear she would sail without us.

One dark night as we sat on the dock, watching the ship's lights, a figure crept toward us. It was Peaches.

"Don't say a word," he whispered, looking around cautiously. "Follow me."

We held our breaths and crept after him down the dock and over the gangplank, onto the ship. It was very dark.

"Go down here. I'll look after you," he whispered, raising a hatch. We disappeared into the yawning hole and found ourselves clinging to a ladder. Peaches closed the hatch, and we were alone. We descended, slowly and cautiously, and finally reached the bottom. We could not see a thing. We tried to feel around us with our hands. Every motion we made was cautious, slow, and quiet. We were afraid to make the least noise. Bandi took my head in his hands, pulled it close to his mouth, and whispered excitedly:

"Don't breathe so loud!" I held back my breath as much as I could.

Slowly our eyes became accustomed to the darkness and we sensed that the hold was very large and filled with cargo. In one part of the hold we discovered some hard, odorless mineral, which Bandi said must be magnesite. In the other part, carbide. We did not have to see it. The smell was unmistakable. Never in my life had I smelled so much carbide all at once. I wondered what anybody could want with so much of it.

There was enough space between the two cargoes to stand up or lie down, as we pleased. After a while we felt, or imagined we felt, that the ship had started. We were not certain about it; but later on the movement was unmistakable. We held each other's hands tightly, and could hardly keep ourselves from screaming with happiness.

Our ship had started toward America! It was dark and smelly and uncomfortable, but it was heaven!

I don't know how many hours passed before our extreme joy gave way to its reaction. It was very difficult to be so happy and remain quiet at the same time. What were we going to do those many, many weeks in this hellhole? I wondered whether the endurance I had bragged about so confidently would be strong enough to cope with the situation. How would I be able to stand this place, the darkness, the silence, for so many weeks? Perhaps we would go insane from fright and worry. And what about food? How would Peaches feed us? He might forget all about us; or he might be unable to bring food. We became terribly hungry.

The actual raw hunger itself did not bother us much, but the thoughts that went with it did. We lost track of time completely. Perhaps Peaches was sick; perhaps he was dead or had forgotten all about us. We would starve before we could reach America!

Perhaps bored workmen would find our corpses, between the magnesite and the carbide. Perhaps silk-shirted American miners would light their lamps with our bones, and wonder angrily what was wrong with their carbide lamps.

I remembered having read in a book by Upton Sinclair, translated into Hungarian, that an average man could go without food for three weeks. The ship would reach American in thirty-three days. According to the book, one had to stop eating in a certain way, which neither of us could remember. But what if we could do so correctly? There was only one way to start fasting so far as we could see.

In spite of our worry and excitement, we fell asleep. When I awoke, I did not know whether I was dreaming or not. I was sleepy, but my eyes were open, and I felt something soft move across my face. Soft hair touched my cheeks. Two small eyes looked at me; threatening, glittering eyes. I did not dare to move or utter a sound. I was spellbound with terror. Then I heard the sound; a whining, terrible sound. I screamed in reply and waved my hands desperately, stamped my feet, and frightened the thing away. It was a rat. An ugly, disgusting, wet, ill-smelling, dirty, grown-up, well-fed rat. A Rat. God! The place it had touched with its mustache burned. It would leave a mark and burn forever.

Rats! Horrible, ugly, big rats! Dangerous rats! The ugliest creatures on earth! The personification of filth! Bandi was shivering with me. We remembered stories in which rats had eaten up innocent people. Should we go up to the captain and complain? Should we tell Peaches that we had tried our best, but we had not been prepared for anything as awful as this? Should we lose everything at the last moment? No. We must stay! We must! We must, if it was possible. But it seemed impossible, humanly impossible. I could not stand rats. I could not! I was willing to face hunger, danger; I was willing to risk my bones by picking fights with husky Italians. I was not a coward, but I could not stay with rats! I loathed them! I choked with the hysterical screams I forcibly stopped in my throat. Another rat swished by my feet. And another one in the corner! I could not stand it any longer. I opened my mouth wide to scream. But Bandi jumped at me and put his hand over my mouth. He shook me; he talked to me as though he were shouting, but soundlessly. His face was distorted as he shouted at me in silent whispers.

"Paul! Paul! I am with you. Stop it! Stop it! We'll go mad! Force yourself to listen to reason. Small animals should not frighten you so much. We are going to America! Would a dirty rat keep us back? No, Paul, no! We'll be sent back if you scream. Please, Paul, stop shivering. Force yourself to stop this shivering; stiffen your muscles. We are going to America. Peaches will lose his job if they find us. It would be ungrateful to him!"

I stiffened. A rat ran by. I looked at it with horrified eyes. Damn Peaches! Damn him! The dirty brute! That's why he lured us here! He knew that we couldn't stand it. He should have known that I was lying to him when I boasted of my ability to suffer. I had been joking. I had been exaggerating, as one would in a situation like that. But he should not have taken it literally! The stupid beast! And I did not say that I could live with rats for weeks and weeks! He should have known that I dreaded rats! Dread them more than lions! There is nothing on earth I dread as much as rats! And he lured us here. I should run up and kill him. The dirty beast!

Bandi whispered to me for hours and hours about rats. They were only small animals; no reason to be afraid of them, to hate them so hysterically, to forego America, glorious America, on account of some little rats! He thought it was ridiculous. The voyage would be over, oh, so soon, he assured me; and we would have a wonderful life ahead of us—without rats. What was the company of a few rats for a few weeks, when the result would be America?

Bandi did everything possible to soothe me. Well, I decided not to mind them—very much. We were going to America, and if we could only go with rats, then with rats we would go.

We slept alternately after that, and every moment while we slept we started awake, frightened, looking for rats. They had a nasty habit of walking leisurely across our faces, hanging to our fingers by their teeth, making aggravating little noises with their nibbling. We held long conferences about the situation, but we could not think of any practical solution. We continued to suffer, but time and experience taught us something. The solution came suddenly and, like all great inventions and discoveries, accidentally.

A certain rat that Bandi had named Hugo B. Bimsenstein became very fresh, and no matter how often Bandi frightened him away, he came back to us, seeking our company, making our lives miserable. This rat was larger and uglier than his fellow rats, and it was easy to pick him out of the crowd. We hated him. Bimsenstein came close to us one day and Bandi angrily grabbed him by the neck. He held him very tightly and Mr. Brimsenstein felt very uncomfortable. He remained motionless, stretched out, looking at us nervously, blinking his small eyes. Bandi tightened the grip on his neck, and dashed Hugo against the magnesite.

Later on, I tried the same thing, forcing myself to touch the ugly and slippery rats! But no matter how hard I threw them they just became dizzy for a while, and then recovered and walked away. After I found this out, I gave any rat I happened to catch to Bandi, and he did the rest.

Such a ship!

Our hunger became greater and greater, but we waited. Bandi said, "Perhaps we think a long, long time has passed since we came here, but it is possible that we came only a day ago."

One night, or day, we were awakened by a noise above our heads. Perhaps somebody had heard me shriek about the rats. Perhaps we had been discovered. It was someone opening the hatch. We almost crawled into the magnesite to hide ourselves. A yellow streak of light shot down into our gloomy temporary home, and we heard Peaches's voice, whispering, "Silence . . . it's me."

He threw down some crackers and dried fish. I took a chance and whispered, "How long have we been here?"

"Two days," he said.

Before he left, Peaches gave us a heavy iron rod to defend ourselves against the rats. Life began to look more pleasant. Bandi could kill any rat who dared disturb us.

The meals we received from Peaches were always a great thrill, and we talked about them for hours.

"You see, we can depend on him. He would not forget us." Bandi said happily.

Darkness . . . darkness . . . the noise of the water as the ship plowed forward; rat-hunting and killing rats with an iron rod. Our amusements were limited.

For hours and hours we remained silent, not knowing what to say to each other. But slowly and surely the ship was going forward every minute, always nearer and nearer to America.

We had not been long together in the hold before we found out everything about our respective families and personal experiences. When those topics were completely exhausted, we told stories to each other, stories we had read.

Darkness . . . the eternal movement of the ship. The monotonous swish of water as the ship proceeded. Fights with rats. Water and food from Peaches almost every day. We praised him, but it did not take long to say everything we had to say about him. A nice man, damn it, a very nice man, but this voyage would never end, never . . . never! As long as we lived, always and without a moment's rest, we would hear the splashing of the water, the whining of the rats, always . . . always.

We had been in the hold five days. I felt that I could not stand it any longer. The darkness; the stealthy movements of the rats, which I could not see, but only sense; the splashing of the water as though it were ready to rush over and swallow us; darkness; rats; the swishing of the waves; and again; and again. No, I did not want to go to America. No country could be worth as much as we were paying. I did not want to become rich and successful. I did not want to be anybody. . . .

Charley had been right to leave me.

I tried to cheer myself by thinking what it would be like to be in the hold alone. The mere thought made me shiver. I would go mad, no doubt of that. It was marvelous to be with Bandi and not alone. And even as it was, the monotony of life in the hold was unbearable at times. It seemed that it would never end.

Bandi invented a game.

"Who was the father of Pallas Athena?" he would ask me.

"Zeus," I would answer.

"And who was Pallas Athena's mother?"

"She had no mother. She jumped out of Zeus's head."

I had won. He was tireless in asking me questions about Greek mythology and other subjects, and often I did not know the answer.

"Who was the father of Hercules?" He wanted to know.

I should have worried. I could not remember. I thought: *Hercules was a very strong man; that was why he was called Hercules. But his family? God only knew. Who cares? Mythology is nothing but a fake, anyway. They were not real people or real gods. Childish! If he had a father, God bless him; if he did not, it was neither his fault nor is it my business.* The trip would not last much longer now. We would soon be in America. Perhaps we still had twenty odd days. Perhaps just twenty. That was not so terrible. Galley slaves were chained to their seats for life. Their situation was much worse than ours. We could count the days, and some day the trip would be over. I should worry about Hercules. Ridiculous! Peaches would come with food, and we would be safely able to say one more day was over.

I could not stand it any longer and burst out, "For heaven's sake, who *was* Hercules' father?"

Bandi would not tell me, but made me think more. It was a very aggravating game. But no matter how hard I tried not to think about it, I had to keep my mind on Hercules, or Hera, or some other god or goddess.

About ten days had passed. Longer than ten years . . . and then we started the counting game. We counted how many more days we had left. . . . How many more hours . . . minutes, seconds. I had to stop this game, for after some hours I noticed that I was not counting hours and minutes, but rats. I caught myself saying, "Seventy-three hundred rats multiplied by twenty-four. . . ." I was on the verge of insanity. But I knew it was up to me to keep my mental balance. I always caught myself in time. When the least thing would have pushed me into chaos, I always saved myself at the last moment by realizing the danger, and by constantly reminding myself that it was up to me: that I would not go mad if I did not want to.

Long deadly silences followed our games. We were tired of each other, tired of America, the ship, Peaches, everything. Perhaps it would be better to end it all. This everlasting voyage would never be over. It seemed that as the days passed, more days stood before us. Days that were long; very, very long. It was hard to commit suicide, though, for we were far below the surface of the water and it was impossible even to jump into the ocean.

Day and night, which meant the same to us, we could hear the splashing of the water. Our existence became timeless . . . and placeless. We were nowhere; very far from the past and just as far from the future. Eight more days. . . . Eternity eight times. . . . We were hardly able to remember how we had lived just a few months before, if it were true at all that we had lived. . . . I had a mother and father, brother and sister. . . . They lived in a comfortable house. Had I ever lived with them? I? This filthy, dirty, unshaven, blinking, half insane creature that I was? If my mother could have seen me like this, she would have died.

They slept in soft, clean beds. . . . Beds had white sheets. Did I know at all what "white" meant? Whiteness? Was there such a thing as *white?* They had a bathroom, a spotless clean bathroom. And I had not washed for twenty-five days. I was filthy. I was crying. I longed for a bath, a white bathtub filled with water, and a bar of white soap; fluffy white towels to caress my body. Water, water—to clean myself! I was dying for water, in the middle of the ocean.

They ate different foods. It was hard to believe that every blessed day they had different food. Meat: big, crisp, juicy pieces to bite into. Soft green vegetables. Bread. And here: dried fish and crackers, dried fish and crackers, and dried fish and crackers. Their table was set with a white tablecloth and they had napkins, white ones, fresh every day. My clothes smelled so desperately of dried fish. I had long whiskers. Sometimes, back then, when I had had a chance to do so, I had not shaved every day! How foolish people were! If I ever came near a bathtub I'd jump into it and remain in it for days and days—and shave over and over again.

They ate with forks and knives, glittering silver forks and knives. And I had been unhappy there! I had wanted to go away! I hated Peaches.

Another day passed, for we had received food again. Seven days more. One week. Only one week more. Darkness, rats, and approaching insanity. I was sure that when the seventh day came I would have heart failure and die.

Sometimes our minds went blank. We did not care about the passing of time. We had no energy left to hope for anything; we had stopped thinking. We knew only that we were in a dark place, that we were dirty, unkempt, and forsaken. Nothing existed outside of the hold; no reminiscences of our past lives, our clean, comfortable, sunny lives; no hopes and dreams about America. Life had stopped for us. Sometimes I thought I was dead already, and this was the nonexistence of afterlife; or else it was our punishment, because we had dared and dreamed.

And then one day Peaches came by and did not give us food. He opened the hold and told us to come up. The ship was floating on just as it always had, and it seemed that it would keep floating on forever and ever. We obeyed wearily. Perhaps he had to give us up to the captain. We were tired; nothing mattered.

The night was silent. Peaches was on duty, and nobody was visible on the deck. Peaches said, "Tomorrow we'll be in New York. I'll put you in my cabin for tonight."

We had two hours of freedom on the deck. We became dizzy and intoxicated, we ran around the deck, trying to outcry the warm summer wind, the American wind!

Bandi noticed the mast, which stood darkly in the night. He gave me a quick look and started to climb it.

I followed him. In a few minutes we were at the top, looking down on the mysterious, deep, dark, roaring, foaming water. The wind blew Bandi's long bushy hair, as he clung there, on top of the world, holding himself with strong arms to the ropes.

Silence—beautiful, speaking, deep silence, underlined with the roaring of the ocean. Then Bandi, first just murmuring to himself, then louder and louder, began to recite a poem about a ship that flew to new seas, a dream ship that went toward new people, and he shouted, yelled, screamed, cried, and sang at the top of his deep voice in feverish ecstasy, as if heralding himself to the whole world.

And our ship went slowly toward America!

It was a beautiful night—an American night.

And then we sensed that our ship was motionless. The journey had ended, so it seemed.

We were in America! We had reached America! New York! Dream of dreams!

Peaches took us up to the deck from his cabin and we looked toward the city of New York that lay before us.

For a minute I held my breath, then I realized that I must have gone insane. I looked around carefully. I watched myself; I decided to manage things without anybody noticing what had happened to me. I knew I was insane.

For there was New York before me, decorated with millions of flags, illuminated with myriad lights; colored lights, sparkling lights, dancing lights, jumping lights; the reckless, unrestricted, crazy fantasy of a pyromaniac! Yes, I was insane. Perhaps those days in the hold—the darkness—the rats—Hercules. . . . Maybe. . . . I didn't know.

"President Wilson will wait for you at the dock . . . the country's best orators . . . young virgins dressed in white . . . and New York will be decorated with millions of flags . . . and illuminated for your arrival. . . ." My father's prediction resounded in my head.

"Lights . . . lights . . . millions of lights!" I heard Bandi murmur.

Then it was true. It must be true. God! You omnipotent and indescribable and undecipherable God! What shall I say to Thee in my happiness and gratitude? America! New York! Bandi was crying.

The day we arrived in America was the fourth of July, nineteen hundred and twenty.

CHAPTER 8

PEACHES TOLD US we would have to go to the city alone, as he would be busy on the boat. He gave us five dollars, and said that we might return it to him when we were rich. And he added, "Now you can go and talk all you want between yourselves about me. . . . A rotter I was to let you starve and suffer in the hold with the rats, eh? I don't care. You can talk as much as you want."

"Peaches," I said, embracing him, "Peaches, I don't know how—"

"Here, have some cigarettes," he said brusquely. He did not like sentimental scenes, being a sentimental man himself.

Following Peaches's instructions, we left the ship. As we started to go toward the city, we were stopped by a tall man who looked like a typical American detective, like those we had seen in the movies. He wore a slouch cap and had a big black cigar stuck in a corner of his mouth. He stood darkly in front of us and raised his hand to stop us. It was only with a great effort that I kept myself from fainting. Everything was lost, I thought. This was a detective, and now that we had practically succeeded, we would be deported. There was no use fighting anymore. He asked us something in English. We did not understand, but I took a desperate chance and answered, "Walking. . . ." It was a word we had learned from

Peaches, and I said it as perfectly as possible. I looked up at the stranger.

"Walking," I said again, but without conviction.

The stranger disregarded our explanation, and slowly put his arms around me. He felt my pockets. Was it a gun he was looking for? And then he let me loose. He searched Bandi, who was frightened and embarrassed, too. Strange country! The man said something again, and let us go. We stood there, white and shivering. We were going to be deported. The man pushed us forward and said, "No whiskey?"

We understood both words. So he was looking for whiskey. Perhaps we were not going to be deported, after all. Slowly, very slowly, in case he might want to shoot, we went forward, and soon found ourselves walking on the streets of New York, America. The detective was forgotten.

This was America—New York. A New York street. . . . Stores with strange, unreadable signs, offering vegetables and all sorts of familiar merchandise, but calling them by strange names. *Cabbage,* a nice word. I wondered what it could mean. It sounded a little bit French. Almost unconsciously I looked at the signs, searching for the American words I had learned from books. *Tomahawk*? I couldn't find it.

Houses, American apartment houses. Nothing extraordinary about them. They were higher than the highest buildings in Budapest, of course. I loved them. They looked strange to me, for inside them were people who talked a language I did not understand. How would a foreigner order a meal in a restaurant? The thought was a bit terrifying. So many people, and none to whom we could talk.

To the first man who came along I showed the business card my uncle had given me in Budapest. He said something

I could not understand and pointed with his finger. We looked at the finger and followed the direction. After a few steps we asked somebody else, and watched him carefully, even making a terrific effort to understand the language, which was perfectly strange to us.

I began to talk big to Bandi. I began to be enthusiastic about America, the dream of our dreams; about our being here, in New York! But I was tired and exhausted, and Bandi had a toothache.

"New York!" I yelled to Bandi to cheer him up, but he was stubborn.

"I have a toothache, and I can't think of anything else. It hurts something awful."

I realized that even in America a toothache is bad, and I felt sorry for Bandi. Here was the biggest thrill of our lives, and I was tired, and he had a bad tooth!

Because we did not know the language, it took us hours to find my uncle's office. We did not dare to take a cab, for we had only the five dollars Peaches had given us, and, in a city as big as New York, a cab might cost any amount.

When we found my uncle's office, I was ready to drop from exhaustion. As we entered, I noticed that the cashier immediately closed the door to the heavy safe in the corner. In our ragged clothes, torn shoes, and slightly dirty faces, we weren't a lovely sight. I went to the cashier, who was a short, middle-aged, and unfriendly man.

"Do you speak Hungarian?" I asked him in that language.

"Yes," he replied, "what do you want?"

"I would like to see the publisher of the paper."

"Sorry, he is in Kentucky."

"How much does it cost to get there?" I asked with a sinking heart.

"One hundred dollars."

We had five.

"When is he coming back?"

"Maybe next winter," said the man, discouragingly.

Bandi and I held a short conference. The cashier turned away. He gave terse instructions to a clerk, completely ignoring us, and answering only when it was absolutely necessary. We stood there helplessly, and were ready to go out somewhere to find a friendly face, when Bandi turned to the hostile man and said to him, "Listen, here is a business card. The publisher of this paper is my friend's uncle. He told him when he was in Budapest to look him up. Is there any way we can get in touch with him?"

The man's face changed as if by magic. The cashier turned into one big smile. He sent a wire to my uncle immediately and took us upstairs to Martin's hotel. We were left alone.

There were two beds in the room, two white beds, with real pillows and clean, white sheets. Bandi's eyes were full of tears as he looked at them. They were so white they dazzled me. The man told me the bathroom was at the end of the hall.

Bathroom!

"You take a bath first," I told Bandi. I was sorry for him for having a toothache on such a glorious occasion. But he resented my offer, and finally we drew lots for the privilege of the first bath. Luckily, Bandi won and he remained in the bathroom for an hour. When he reappeared he was shaved, clean and fresh, a new Bandi. His tooth had even stopped aching. It was good to look at him.

Then I, in turn, shaved off my five weeks' beard with an American razor, looked at myself in the mirror—a new person, someone I had never seen before, an immigrant; a European immigrant in America. I stepped into the bathtub and let the water run. More and more clean water for my poor neglected body. I reveled in the clear, cold water. Only the rushing noise it made, reminiscent of the boat, irritated me a little.

Then the bed, the dear, beautiful, white bed. My whole body ached with the accumulated aches of thirty-three days, which I was feeling now for the first time. I thanked God many times, very sincerely, for allowing me to leave that ship and lie in a clean bed, an American bed.

We fell asleep immediately. I don't know how long I slept, but I had a horrible dream just before I awoke. I dreamed that a gigantic rat was about to rush at me, and as I tried to jump away, I had that sensation of falling, falling. . . . I awoke and found Bandi, all dressed, sitting on the bed, waiting for me. I was happy, dizzy with happiness.

It was morning.

"Come on, Paul, they are waiting for us at the office. They have received a telegram from Martin, and they'll buy us new suits, shoes, and everything."

An uncle!

CHAPTER 9

WEARING CLEAN LINEN, new suits, and shoes, Bandi and I, two immigrants, walked on the American streets. Yes, this was America, and everybody spoke English, an utterly strange language. Even the little children! I had had plenty of time to learn English in Budapest. Why hadn't I?

In Martin's office we were given the address of a Hungarian restaurant on Second Avenue. We were surprised at the thickly populated and noisy streets. Millions of children played on the ill-smelling pavement. And the side streets with pushcarts and rags and stinking food! But it was New York—Heaven—just the same. We opened our eyes wide to take in every color and every line, and we drank in the noises, American noises—a peculiar, disturbing, and fantastic unharmonious harmony. Our Hungarian voices, our Hungarian exclamation, and expressions of surprise and joy, were already a part of the concert of the New York streets. We belonged. Residents of New York. . . .

We stepped in to the restaurant and heard Hungarian words here and there, mixed with Hungarianized English words. I felt like running to each table where my countrymen were sitting and shouting my name to them, announcing to them that I was here. I had arrived to stay, to live with them.

Nobody paid any attention to us. We sat down at a table, and I heard Bandi choke. He was staring at the table. I looked and choked too. There was sugar on the table, a whole bowl full of fine, snow-white sugar. We had not seen white sugar for years in Hungary. The war and the revolutions had made our country very poor. We had brown sugar, and not enough of that. . . .

We ordered Wiener Schnitzel, for the bill of fare was written in English, and that was the only item we understood. And then the waiter brought us bread in a little basket, without asking us for a bread ticket! Bread! Many, many slices of white bread, and rolls, half a dozen of them! We hadn't seen white bread and rolls for years. We were stunned. I bit savagely into the crisp roll. Bandi's eyes shone as he said, "This is peace, Paul. . . . This is the first time I have realized that the war is over. This roll gives me that taste of peace I have yearned for so long."

Bandi was right. To eat a roll, white bread, and to have a bowl of sugar on the table, that was peace. Yes, the war had ended long ago, but our poor country was cursed with one revolution after another, the continuation of war. The Great War had moved from the trenches into the middle of the city. Poverty reigned over Budapest, which had once been so carefree and prosperous. Yes, this was peace. And we were here, in the country of peace and prosperity.

"Listen," said Bandi, after lunch, "I have an idea that we can even buy as many cigarettes as we feel like."

It sounded unbelievable, but it was so. They gave us two packages of cigarettes without asking for our tobacco ticket, and without even looking at us suspiciously.

"I feel like a king," said Bandi, as we walked along the street, with the contentment of well-fed people, smoking good cigarettes. I laughed.

"That's a poor comparison. How does a poor king feel nowadays? I'll tell you how to feel. You feel like an American resident, Mister Vida."

And throughout the day we addressed each other as 'Mister.' We were full of enthusiasm and love of life. We felt that we were going to conquer this country; how, we did not bother to figure out. We were full of energy, ready to tackle the impossible. We asked for a dictionary at the office, and went up to our room and started to learn English. The first evening we learned to count up to twenty, and the names of the days of the week. And the next day, while speaking Hungarian, we never missed the chance to say any and all numbers in English.

I was in a constant daze, absolutely unable to make clear observations. I hardly had time to wonder at one thing when my attention was attracted to another marvel. Often I had the feeling that I was dreaming, and would hear a knock, and then my father's voice saying, "Paul, get up." My impressions had the characteristics of dreams; they were chaotic. My reactions changed every minute.

I felt joy in looking at the skyscrapers. I felt sudden fear in riding on the subway. I was amazed to see that the elevated trains did not run on the tops of the apartment houses, as we had imagined in Europe. I was discouraged on hearing the English language spoken glibly everywhere; and I felt elated upon seeing my reflection in show windows, behind foreign words. I was disappointed on finding out what *cabbage* meant, and that it was pronounced without any French flavor; and I was thrilled as I wandered in a five and dime store.

Bandi screamed when we saw a pushcart full of oranges, for they were forbidden fruit in our country, labeled "luxury." Only millionaires could afford to have one or two smuggled into the country from Italy. I ate bananas reverently—that exotic fruit, so rare in our country. I wondered at the people who chewed for hours on chewing gum, something absolutely unknown to me. I was desperate when I found many Hungarians who had been in America ten years and still spoke the language imperfectly.

How strange it was for me, having come from Hungary, to see so many colored people in regular clothes, walking along the streets. In Europe I had seen them only in circuses. I was touched on seeing the Fire Department give free baths on the streets to the children of the overpopulated East Side. I almost cried when I was unable to open the window, for even the windows were so very different from European French windows. I was sorry for the Americans who ate their lunches standing at a counter; sorry for them because the stores were not closed for two hours at noon, so that the employees might have a leisurely lunch and an hour at the café. I was bewildered in the drugstore, where they sold handkerchiefs and food and drinks and toys and stationery and stamps and newspapers and cigarettes. I was pleasantly surprised to see that all the girls wore silk stockings, which in Budapest were worn only by stage stars and the very rich.

To watch the evening rush around the subway stations was breath-taking. I could not understand why everyone hurried on the streets. In Budapest people walked to their destinations. Our streetcars, horse-drawn carriages, and automobiles moved leisurely, giving the passenger time to enjoy the ride; here, riding seemed to be a very inconvenient, unpleasant necessity.

The Capitol Theatre, a motion picture house, dazzled me. The huge orchestra played the *William Tell Overture* with a realistic lightning effect at the storm scene, to my amazement.

I was not able to untangle my impressions from the chaos that reigned in my mind. I could not imagine which would be the strongest one, the lasting one. I could not see the future, and could not answer the many disturbing questions that came to my mind.

Could I learn the language? Could I rush and run as others did? Could I eat a light lunch standing at a counter? Could I become a full-fledged American? Or would I forever remain an amazed and wondering stranger? Could I spend years here to fight for success? And would I ever succeed? Would I write home for money, and return, beaten, to Budapest in a few months? And . . . was there a girl in the crowd, in that dense, rushing crowd, who was meant for me, who would love me and understand me? Or would I send money to Klari and bring her over?

I didn't know, I didn't know. All those questions, all the uncertainty, disturbed and bewildered me, but made me happy just the same. For I was in the center of life's vortex, and things were going to happen to me; and that was what I wanted; change, wide perspectives, possibilities, unlimited possibilities.

CHAPTER 10

Bandi and I were sitting in a little lunchroom across from the office one morning, eating breakfast, when a young woman entered. She was plainly, almost severely dressed, but with an indescribable touch of individuality in her style. Since the lunchroom was full, she sat at our table, and reached out for the menu. The first thing I noticed was her hand, her long, slender fingers, with pointed nails, wearing an old, hand-wrought silver ring, set with a huge black stone.

"Poison," was the word that struck me as I looked at the extraordinary hand. My voice vibrated with excitement as I said to Brandi, in Hungarian:

"Please look at this woman at our table. I don't dare to, myself. I love her hand, and I am afraid that she is ugly."

A little silence, then Bandi said, "You can look up, she is not ugly."

But still I hesitated, asking, "Is she beautiful?"

"No," he replied, "she is not beautiful."

I looked up. She was not beautiful. She was pale and dark, and she was sad; not momentarily sad, but a profound sadness was expressed around her mouth. She had large, deep black eyes, bottomless pits. An interesting, fascinating, breathtaking person. I looked at her, and I was aware that my eyes were expressing my admiration freely and abundantly.

Without any reason at all, I became sad also, and started to talk to her, turning my head a little toward Bandi. I spoke in Hungarian, which I was certain she would not understand. I felt that I must tell her something.

"You girl, with those beautiful hands, how I would like to talk to you; for I have so much to say to you. You girl, with those heartrending, sad eyes that seem to hide the torture of suffering, why are you American, knowing only the savage English language, when there are poems written in Hungarian, written to you and for you, dedicated to your eyes?"

And I continued whispering words to Bandi, words I spoke for her, and I thought that she must know that I was talking to her, for she looked at me for a single second. When she finished her breakfast, I was reciting Hungarian poetry to her, a love poem, in which the poet called his sweetheart a queen, telling her that the gilded equipage waited to take her, the queen, with him, the king, among the people, to be worshipped: and the last line described the sad awakening from the dream. At this moment the woman at our table arose, and with a very faint, almost sad smile, turned toward me and said. slowly, ". . . and the old cab stumbled, stumbles, and we tremble and shiver . . ."

She said it in perfect Hungarian, in a velvety low voice, and that sad tone indicating perfect understanding of the poem. And then she went to the cashier, paid her check, and left the place.

Bandi and I sat there, amazed. What was it? Was it a hallucination? Had my ears tricked me? Or was she really Hungarian? I jumped up and ran out, and Bandi, after paying the check, ran out after me. There were a few people on the street, but the girl had vanished. We kept running around the block, looking into stores and houses, but the girl had disappeared as if the earth had swallowed her. Perhaps she hadn't even existed. Had my imagination created her? But Bandi had seen her, too.

There we stood on the street, desperate and bewildered, talking about her, trying to verify her existence. We compared descriptions of her. Our impressions coincided exactly. This was proof that she really was, and that she had been sitting at our table and had finished my Hungarian poem.

I had to go to the office. There was nothing to be gained by lingering there on the corner, but I asked Bandi to look around, and if he could find the girl, he must get acquainted with her somehow; he must not hesitate to risk anything. We had to know her.

I entered the office and the stenographer told me that the paper's managing editor had returned from vacation and wanted to talk to me. I was prepared to tell him immediately that I did not like the paper very much, and had several ideas about changes, which would certainly please my uncle, for I had been a newspaper writer in Budapest and felt I knew how to make a paper. I went into the office with a superior air.

A woman was sitting at the desk, smoking a cigarette. She turned toward me with a ready, polite smile that froze on her face immediately. And I . . . I closed my eyes, for I was sure that they were tricking me. Then a long, slender hand reached toward me, and in a moment my lips were pressed to it, and I felt the cool stone of the ring against my face.

We looked at each other, utterly confused, and then she smiled and said, "Of course you could not have known that there are so many Hungarians in New York; everywhere, in fact. It is not very advisable to make remarks about anyone aloud."

"Are you angry with me?" I stammered.

"Of course not," she answered, "I love the poem you recited, and you did it very nicely. I might have guessed that you were the nephew with whom I am ordered to be very strict. I spent my vacation at your uncle's place, and he appointed me your guardian. He does not believe in making his nephew's life too easy. He instructed me to make you work hard, harder than anybody else, in fact, and he also instructed me to fire you if you do not work diligently. So you had better behave yourself. Now, I have to go to the printing shop, and you might read the issues of the past few months to become acquainted with the paper—for of course I don't expect you to know much about America's miners—and, next week, perhaps you can try your hand at an article."

She left the office, and I stood there staring after her. I was happy at finding her but was furious with her. What did she mean by telling me to behave myself? I decided that as soon as she came back I would go to her office and tell her that I was not a child, did not propose to behave myself, and so on. But she was so busy all day, for she was also the business manager of the paper, conferring with advertising men, dictating letters, writing articles, quarreling with the printers, that I could not find an occasion to talk to her. A few minutes before closing time I decided to go to her office, as soon as the stenographer left.

The stenographer came out, and told me that the editor wanted to see me. I went in.

She was putting on her hat, and said in a matter-of-fact voice, "I'd be glad if you would have dinner with me. I have a Hungarian cook. I imagine that American food is rather hard on you."

I went home with her. She had a most interesting apartment: a huge room; an immense couch in a corner, covered with some sort of black material and strewn with dozens of colorful cushions; book shelves with hundreds of Hungarian books by the best authors, the most modern ones, my favorites. The table was set with Hungarian peasant dishes, and we ate Hungarian food. Could I be rude to her and tell her what I thought about being bossed around? In her own home, at her own dinner table? I decided to wait until after dinner, and then tell her, though of course not rudely, but firmly. After dinner, however, we talked of other things, and I simply couldn't switch the subject to fit in with my little speech. It was midnight when I left.

Bandi was in bed when I reached our room. He wasn't asleep. When I came in he said, sadly, "I didn't find her," and he described at great length a dozen schemes to find her. After he had finished telling me his wildest idea, I said, "She is my boss, the editor of my uncle's paper."

I did not tell him much more that night. I could not sleep. I loved America; and, after all, I thought, she was right . . . certainly I should behave myself. . . . Perhaps I would.

The next day phrases that Yelena had spoken came back to my mind: "No matter how much money you make, you must save a certain amount every week," or, "In America you must work hard. It is worthwhile."

She said that she was telling me facts and was not interested in my opinion, if any. I was frightened somehow, and could not figure out why. Was I afraid of something or somebody? Certainly not. But still I had that strange, scared-to-death feeling. And the feeling was definitely connected with the girl I had met. Her name was Yelena . . . Slavic . . . Her mother was a Slav, and she represented an interesting and mysterious mixture of Slavic and Hungarian ancestry. She seemed to like me; she had taken a great interest in me. I was sure that she would play a very important part in my life. Perhaps I would have to suffer a great deal on her account. Oh, nonsense! Suffer! The minute I wanted to, I could dismiss her. Who was she, anyway? A stranger.

What did she mean about saving money? Who cared about saving? I had no use for thrift. And it did not sound sincere, the way she said it. Yet, come to think of it, it was not such a bad idea, after all. Save first, and then when you have a small amount, start something and be somebody. But beyond saving and beyond everything, her voice was the most important thing about her. Several times that night I had caught myself listening to her voice and not her words; and it was a thrill to hear it. From the next day on I was going to save money.

I went to the office. At frequent intervals during the day I found excuses to go into her office to ask unnecessary questions about our work, just to hear her voice. We went out for lunch together and she took me to the bank where I deposited my first savings in America—five dollars. She seemed thrilled.

Before leaving the office, at five o'clock, she said to me, "If you behave nicely, little boy, I'll take you to Greenwich Village and other nice places next Sunday."

I remembered in the office, wondering, and then I worked myself up to a rage. What did she mean, "behave nicely?" Was I a child, an infant? The idea! "Behave!" How was I to "behave nicely"? She had to be insane to talk that way to me. And that bank business irritated me, too. She was treating me as though I were a child, a schoolboy. I was supporting myself. And she called me a "Greenhorn" before strangers. I would find out what that word meant. It certainly sounded very low and degrading. I was not a "Greenhorn," whatever that was. How ridiculous!

I was not in love with her!

I was in love with Klari, was I not? If that was love, I was sure I could not be in love with Yelena. Still, it was nice to think about her, playing with the phrase she had spoken, and dreaming of many promising, bright tomorrows. It often happened when I was alone that I suddenly heard her voice calling me, calling my name, definitely and unmistakably; her soft, velvety voice, victoriously breaking through the silence of my room.

I behaved, somehow. I really don't know how it happened, but she told me that the next day we were going to Greenwich Village. Bandi was also invited.

"I want you to see and love America," she said. "If you love her, she will know it and will love you and be kind to you. I am going to show you things. Be at my house with your friend tomorrow evening at seven o'clock, before dinner."

Bandi was enthusiastic about the whole idea, and the next evening we were at her house at fifteen minutes of seven. A strange man was there; six feet tall, very handsome, with an exceptionally intelligent face. I looked at him with suspicious eyes. I didn't like his being there. Yelena introduced him to us as Ivan, her brother, an artist. Brother? Good! We were to be his guests for the evening.

Ivan took us to a French restaurant for dinner. I had never seen such a beautiful place. It was like an illustration from a fairy tale. There were colorful frescoes on the walls. Yelena told me Winold Reiss, a famous German painter, had made them. The table was heavily laden with silver and specially painted dishes, also designed by Reiss. The waiters were elegant, attentive, and quiet, and how they served us! They read our desires in our very eyes. And the food they laid before us looked too beautiful to be eaten. Yelena and Bandi had oysters, a rare and very expensive delicacy, eaten only by millionaires in Hungary. But I did not dare to taste them. It was then that I ate my first olive. Bitter! Looking at the table, food, and waiters, I could not help but remember the dried fish Peaches had thrown down to us.

"We wouldn't have much of a chance to make money by singing here," Bandi remarked. He, too, was remembering.

From the restaurant we went in a cab, to the Ziegfeld Follies, of which I had heard so much in Europe. Girls? No, angels! Dancing, singing, heavenly decorations, a whirl of colors, rainbow-rich silks. Girls, girls, girls. Jewelry, the revelry of motion and color and sound in perfect harmony. And around us, in the audience, ladies in evening gowns, jeweled white throats, and gentlemen in tuxedos: that very good-looking American type of gentleman, a little gray at the temples. I had thought they existed only in illustrations.

Perhaps I was dreaming. Could it be true that in such a very few days we had emerged from the rats and dirt to this exhibition of wealth and happiness? But Bandi was there with me, and so too were Yelena and Ivan. It was true!

We went to the Biltmore Hotel roof for ice cream and coffee. It was true, then, that in New York there were cafés and restaurants on the tops of the buildings. A colored fountain bubbled in the center of the room. We sat next to it. Somewhere, hidden by palms, an orchestra played, and many well-dressed, good-looking couples danced. Even the elderly couples were fresh and young in spirit. Yelena and Bandi danced. I watched them, for I couldn't dance, and even if I could, I was too small. Yelena was a tall girl. I sat there with Ivan, speechless, but I think he understood. The whole thing: the introduction to America, as Yelena had put it, made me sad and inarticulate. I was dazed with beauty. I was frightened at seeing, without warning, this magnificence of life, of American life. But it had just the opposite effect on Bandi. His eyes were flashing. His whole being sparkled. He was living every moment consciously, as if absorbing all the beauty in order to keep its memory forever. I was but a dazzled spectator, drunk with rich impressions. Bandi was a living part of the whole miracle, accepting it immediately, stepping into it.

After the Biltmore, another taxi ride through Broadway, and Fifth Avenue, while Brandi yelled his exalted love confessions for New York into the bright night.

We left Fifth Avenue and went through some crooked, old-fashioned streets, and stopped in front of a funny place. It was called Pirate's Den. A wild pirate, dressed in a costume out of the book of adventure of my youth, stood in the doorway, holding a horribly big, rusty sword. Ivan greeted the man, and we went into a dark cellar, and from there, on a squeaky ladder, climbed up to the restaurant. I felt like a young boy who had strayed into a storybook in his dreams.

The inside of the place looked like a pirate ship. On the backs of the chairs were imprints of bloody hands, and the skull and crossbones. Artificial dirt and cobwebs were everywhere. One the tables, candles stuck in bottles, dripped. Waiters were dressed like pirates. One of them even had a black patch over one eye. In the corner were the treasure chests. The restaurant had three floors and an opening in the center, hung with ropes, which the waiters climbed up and slid down, when going from one floor to the other. It was fun. We ate Captain Kidd sandwiches, and walnuts served in a wooden bowl, fashioned to look like a split skull, and smoked Coffin Nail cigarettes. Bandi and Yelena danced again.

Though I had been forewarned, I almost became frightened when I heard a loud noise, and all the waiters started to dash after a man who was running around the place and climbing ropes frantically.

"The prisoner has escaped!" one of the pirates shouted. Finally, after a merry chase, they caught him and chained him. Don Dickerman, the captain, came down from the bridge, looked at the captive with narrowed eyes, and started to shoot him with his rusty old pistol. Then everything became quiet again. Some of the guests—newcomers—were frightened by this bit of play-acting. Dickerman, the owner of the Den, had played his part with the seriousness of a boy.

It was after four in the morning when we left the Pirate's Den and started to walk to Ivan's studio. It was a beautiful dawn, the most beautiful of my life. The sun was fighting with the mist that covered the silhouettes of the skyscrapers. I was ready to cry.

Ivan's studio was an enormous, high room with an open fireplace and a few strange, massive pieces of furniture.

There were pictures all over the walls—Ivan's work. I had never seen such peculiar, beautiful pictures in my life. Yelena was proud to show us her brother's work. Slender, graceful women, with long legs, long arms, and Yelena-like hands. Mythical, sad monks, with everlasting thirst and desire in their eyes. Vivid, breathing colors, batiks, brushes, paints, and a fantastic photograph of Yelena.

Ivan played a violin and sang for us in a deep, warm, pleasant voice while Yelena started to prepare breakfast. I watched her as she put a smock over her evening gown and opened a big closet, which was a miniature, hidden kitchen. She made coffee in an electric percolator, toast in an electric toaster. Then she folded down a little table from the wall, and there was the breakfast: fresh fruit, coffee, toast, jam, and honey. It was delicious.

When we took Yelena home, we couldn't say a word to her. We left her at her house, and remained on the street, Bandi and I. For a long time we walked without saying a word, then suddenly Bandi stopped and threw out his arms, crying to the awakening street:

"New York. . . . Beautiful. . . . Follies. . . . Yelena, beautiful, darling Yelena. . . . Ivan. . . . His studio . . . The whole living, fantastic city here! And it's mine! Mine!!"

I was sad. Well, Yelena had showed me New York. Yes, it was mine too, if . . . if I could conquer it. I would start tomorrow morning, Monday, but how?

CHAPTER 11

I WAS ON the road to prosperity. Every week I saved five dollars, and the total soon amounted to quite a sum if figured in Hungarian money. This, of course, was only the beginning. Yelena was satisfied with me. In a few months, I thought, I might manage to put aside ten dollars a week, and in a few years I might have a thousand dollars saved. Then, with that money in my pocket I could go home, visit my people, and marry Klari.

I had received a letter from her, the first letter. I was trembling as I opened it and read:

Dear Paul,

I was happy to hear that you arrived in America safely. I know you will become a big man there, and probably will forget me. I am at the zoo every single day, working. Your friend Charley came to see me. It was sweet of you to send him. He told me what an interesting life you led in Italy. He is a very nice boy. It would be nice if you would write me often and tell me everything about America and yourself.

Love,

Klari

Was that all? She could have written a much longer letter, I thought. But then I immediately forgave her, for what could the poor thing write about? What did she know about life? She spent her days at the zoo behind a soda counter, waiting on thirsty, unpleasant people. It was nice of Charley to go to see her, though I did not remember having sent him.

I answered her letter immediately. I wrote pages and pages, describing New York, Yelena, that marvelous evening we had together, and my hopes. But I did not send it. Reading it over, I realized that she would feel very unhappy, for the letter gave the impression that my dominant emotion was happiness at being in America, and not unhappiness at being away from her. I was afraid she would not understand. So I wrote another letter, allowing for more pages about my unhappiness and fewer for the description of New York and Yelena.

Bandi came to the office to call for me, and after working hours Yelena began to talk of Bandi's future. In the course of the conversation, she picked up the telephone and asked for a number.

"Hello, George," she said. "Do me a favor? I have a friend here. . . . Yes, he can sing. . . . Very good looking. . . . Thanks, I'll send him to see you tonight."

Yelena gave Bandi an address, and that night he got a job: singing in the chorus of a Broadway theatre. He was to start in a few days. He tried to thank her, but she passed it off lightly and offered to teach him the words of the songs he would have to sing. She also ordered us to study English with her once a week, because the first thing one should do in a strange country is to learn the language, to understand the country, and make oneself understood.

That night we were invited to a studio party at Ivan's. Yelena was there, dressed in a scarlet gown. Two old silver bracelets jingled on her lovely arms. She had a style of her own.

An interesting group was gathered in the big studio: Delly, a tall, black-haired, lazy-bodied painter; Jack, a blond Swedish sculptor of gigantic build, and a Turkish girl, his sweetheart; a young actress with a heart shaped face; a German baroness who wrote poetry in English; a rich and beautiful American girl who was hopelessly in love with Ivan; a Hungarian writer who worked in a factory and was hopelessly in love with Yelena; Rita, an American dancer; a middle-aged American pianist who was even shorter than I, and I liked him for it; and a Russian princess. Ivan pointed out Rita to me, saying, "She is a wonderful dancer, and will dance for us tonight." I was not interested in her. She was not bad looking, but uninteresting, indifferent, as she sat lazily on a couch, in a corner of the room.

I, too, sat in a corner, looking at the people, watching them, enjoying their erratic conversation, though not understanding much of it. Ivan played the violin and sang for us, and when he finished, the victrola was wound up, and everybody danced. Bandi danced most of the time with Yelena, and occasionally with the pretty American girl. *It must be very good to dance,* I thought. *One can be so free.* Rita, I noticed, did not dance with anybody, despite her reputation. Nobody paid much attention to her, until midnight, when Ivan announced that Rita would dance for us. Everyone applauded politely, and sat down on the couches and comfortable chairs scattered around the studio.

Rita wore a loose-fitting dress, and I watched her because there was nothing else to watch. She danced with grace and beauty, and as she finished, everybody applauded enthusiastically.

Then she left the room, only to reappear a moment later clad in nothing but a thin veil. She started to dance, and as she moved, she threw away the veil, and there she was, dancing, her young beautiful, slender body naked. It was a miracle. The girl who was not exceptionally pretty became transformed. Her face, her whole body, was transfigured by the emotional feeling in her dance, and everybody stared at her, men and women alike.

In her dance she symbolized a young and innocent girl who has just met the Man. They become acquainted. . . . He loves her. . . . The first kiss. . . . Desire. . . . The first indescribable sensation. . . . Happiness. . . . She melts and dies from the joy of his arms.

Rita's eyes were half closed as she slowly sank to the floor.

The dance was over. Rita quickly put the veil around her body. She had danced so beautifully that most of the people had forgotten she was naked.

I looked around the studio. My eyes rested on Delly, the artist. He was staring, as if hypnotized, with round, steady eyes, at Rita . . . who returned his gaze. Slowly, Delly went toward the girl. When he was close to her, for a moment, for a long, long moment they looked into each other's eyes. Finally, with a sudden movement, Delly put his arms around her waist and kissed her passionately. Rita returned the kiss, and the man—the happy victor—picked her up and carried her out, undoubtedly to his own studio, which was in the same building. That was the first time they had met.

During the rest of the evening there was singing and dancing, but I couldn't fasten my attention on anything. I was thinking of Rita and Delly.

The party broke up early in the morning. I was blue, somehow, and thinking of Klari. There was I, attending studio parties. I had New York, theatres, movies, friends, Rita, Delly, Yelena; and she led such a colorless, monotonous existence in poor old Budapest serving soda in the zoo to ugly customers.

In a few days Bandi started on his job with a musical comedy on Broadway. I went to see the performance with Yelena and I laughed as I saw Bandi come on the stage, playing the part of a guest in a restaurant who merrily bursts into song. He sang very well.

Every day he had something to say about his new life. He was happy, and always had great hopes and plans for the future. From what he told me, he was the only man in the chorus who had theatrical ambitions. He said most of the other boys dreamed of a successful grocery store or some such business, with a wife and a settled life. They did not have false desires and ambitions. They did not think they were actors: just workingmen who wanted to save money.

Time flew by in New York. There were new happenings, new impressions, new friends, new dreams, new ambitions every day.

One day a very poorly dressed Hungarian man came into our office. He stammered and stalled for time, and finally confessed that he was penniless and had not eaten all day. He had looked desperately for a job, he said, and had not been able to find one. Yelena gave him some money and told him where to go to find work.

I was shocked. It was a strange and almost impossible that a man should have no money and no job, I thought, for one could do things in America. One could work, one could make money, and save. He must be a bum or a good-for-nothing. To me, New York was wealth and happiness.

Yelena, Bandi, Ivan, and I had many long talks about New York and always came to the conclusion that it was the utmost one could wish for in the way of cities.

Bandi liked Yelena very much. He was grateful to her for his job; like me, he admired and adored her for everything she did. For my part, all fear and resentment toward her had disappeared like magic, and I felt an everlasting, dependable, strong affection for her. In fact, I hardly could imagine life without Yelena.

One day rumors began to circulate in the office to the effect that the paper was going to be moved to Kentucky. This went on for a few days. I didn't pay much attention at first, but when I heard it whispered for the fiftieth time, I started to think. How great it would be if Martin should ask me to go, too. In Kentucky I could save more money and would have a chance to be near Martin, who would teach me about the miners and the mines, and some day—who knows—perhaps I would be a mine owner. Almost anything could happen in America. Kentucky. . . . Yelena had been there before I met her. It had to be a good place. I would see those miners with their silk shirts and cars. It would be nice to go.

One day Kentucky became a reality. I received a letter from Martin telling me that he was going to move the paper down to Kentucky, and asking me to come, too. He wrote:

"I cannot promise you much entertainment in this mining town, but here you can learn things, and here you will have a chance to be somebody. If you are not afraid of hard work, come. Wire me your decision immediately."

I showed this letter to Yelena, saying:

"Oh, I'm so glad Martin has asked me to go to Kentucky. I know I'll be happy there. A small town, where I can save lots of money."

"I also have a letter from him," she said, "but I'm not going. I have been there. It's a nice place, but I don't feel like living there."

"Are you going to give up your job?" I asked.

She smiled.

"It looks like it. It doesn't matter."

Then I began to wonder whether I should go to Kentucky or not. Not much diversion there; I knew that much. A silly little mining town with dirty miners. And New York, the big, marvelous city. . . . It certainly would be stupid to leave it. I didn't know anything about mines or miners, and wondered if I could ever learn the business. Would I like it at all? I thought not. Yelena was going to stay in New York. I didn't see why I couldn't get a job if she could. It would be unwise to sacrifice all my chances for Kentucky, of which I knew practically nothing.

I talked it over with Bandi. He thought I should stay in New York. He was right, I thought. I shouldn't have taken this job in the first place. It was too easy to work for my own uncle. This was not the only job I could find in such a gigantic city.

I wrote to Martin explaining that I would not go to Kentucky. He evidently did not like my letter, for his reply read:

> *I really don't want you to come here if you don't want to. But I must tell you frankly that I am disappointed. Apparently you are afraid of the hard work that awaits you here. At first, against my principles, I tried to make your life as pleasant as possible in this country. I see now that I was wrong. This was your big chance, and now, as a disinterested spectator, but not as a helper, I will watch your struggles with life in America. To avoid any embarrassment in the future, I am telling you now, that if you do not come now, you cannot come later.*

Yes, he had made things easy for me, and he shouldn't have. I would do things for myself as a grown man should. I didn't need his interest in me, and I didn't need his help. I would stay in New York!

The paper moved, but Yelena and I remained in New York. In a few days Yelena got a position as assistant editor with another Hungarian paper in New York. I looked for a job every day, but without success. I was glad that I had saved money, for now I needed it. I had almost fifty dollars. Yelena had been right!

I tried to get a job with the same paper, but when they learned that I didn't know English, they wouldn't have me. They told me that the "ticker" was written in English, and I wouldn't be able to read the news.

To save money, I began to take my meals in a small Hungarian restaurant on Tenth Street frequented by poor young people, mostly. They served excellent food and charged very little for it. There I met an elderly man who had come to America twenty years before me. While there one night with Bandi, I was talking to him about my situation, and as I was telling him about the Hungarian paper's refusal to take me because of my lack of English, the strange Hungarian man interrupted me.

"Pardon me," he said, "but I see that you are a greenhorn here. May I give you a piece of good advice?"

I did not want his advice, but before I had a chance to refuse it, the man continued:

"You should not try to get a job with a paper. You should work, otherwise you will never succeed. Greenhorns are peculiar. They never want to listen to an old American. Go and work in a factory. Get some steady American job for yourself. Try to be an American. Save money, and then you are set for the rest of your life!"

I looked at Bandi. We got up from the table and left the place. What nerve he had, telling me what to do! But the truth was that my little money was disappearing fast, and I really didn't know what I would do if something didn't turn up in the very near future.

When Yelena had been working for quite a while in her new position, I went up to see her one day, and we talked for a long time.

"I know a printer," she said, "a very nice man. He is the publisher of a small Hungarian paper in New Brunswick, New Jersey, not far from here. Maybe he can use you there. You wouldn't have to know much English. You could come to New York every other weekend."

I was immensely relieved. How marvelous Yelena was! I had great faith in her, for whatever she started, she invariably succeeded in finishing properly. Perhaps I could get that job. I would be near New York, and it would be a position.

A few days passed, and I began to grow desperate. I did not even look for a job, for I was waiting for the position in New Brunswick. I had completely run out of money, and Bandi was lending me dollars, when one day Yelena told me everything was set for the job. I could go there immediately and take the position.

Yelena and Bandi took me to Pennsylvania Station to see me off.

I didn't like the idea of leaving New York, but there was nothing else to do. I had to go. And anyway, New Brunswick was not really far away. The ticket was only a little more than a dollar, and Yelena told me that I would be there in seventy-five minutes. Just like working way downtown and living way uptown, in New York. The only difference was that the place was called New Brunswick and not New York.

It was hard to say a real goodbye to my friends, for in spite of the tears I saw in both Bandi's and Yelena's eyes, I felt I wasn't seriously going away from New York.

CHAPTER 12

ON THE TRAIN bound for New Brunswick, I began to experience qualms. I had almost the same feeling when I'd left Budapest for Vienna. New people, new faces, new streets, new houses again.

What kind of a man might my boss be? What would my job be? *Ah,* I told myself, *I am a man, serious, dependable and sensible; I can take care of myself anywhere.*

I began to form sentences in my mind. I was thinking of the first letter I would write to Yelena.

When I arrived in the station at New Brunswick I felt a lump rise in my throat. I was not afraid, but I was wondering. This new city, what would it give me? Happiness? Money? Tears? Love? What would happen to me there? Would I succeed or would I fail?

The printer was a small, energetic man of about forty, with a fat, pleasant wife and four children. He had been a soldier in Hungary, and he liked to talk about his experiences in the army. He reared his children with soldierlike discipline, and gave orders in a loud, stern voice. On the whole, however, he was a pleasant man.

He told me all my duties the first day, and I learned that my salary would be fifteen dollars a week to start with. It seemed that we would get along very well. He gave me many old copies of his paper, the *Hungarian News,* and I read them with ambition and interest. I was determined to make good.

Guests frequented the printer's house, and I tried hard to make friends, but it was difficult to interest myself in them. My thoughts were in New York, with Yelena and Bandi. I kept wondering what they were doing.

It was a fine feeling to be at work again after the many endless hours of idleness in New York. The paper kept me quite busy. I discovered I was not only the editor but the business manager and general helper as well. I had to solicit advertisements, write articles, help the printer set up the paper, and run the primitive little machine that cut and pasted the mailing list on the papers. In my idle hours I helped the printer's children with their homework, and in addition to that, I played cards, against my better judgment, with the printer and his brother-in-law. It was hard to save money, for out of my fifteen a week I paid ten dollars for room and board at the printer's house. Still, I was sure to make good and get a raise.

I was an editor, and although my name did not appear on the editorial page, everybody knew it, and in a few weeks, the local Lajos Kossuth Association asked me to give a lecture in their hall on the following Sunday.

I assured them that I would lecture, but when they inquired as to my subject, I was a little embarrassed. I did not know at the moment what I would talk about, but after a little thinking I said that my subject would be, "Unlimited Opportunities for the Foreigner in America."

I had planned to go to New York for the weekend, as I had not seen Bandi and Yelena for a long time, but I had to postpone the trip on account of my lecture.

Greenhorn

The large hall of the Lajos Kossuth Association was crowded. I started my speech.

"We foreigners must like America, and then America will like us also. The most important thing for foreigners in this country is to learn the language, to live a clean, honest life, and save money. One of the greatest Americans, Benjamin Franklin, said, 'A penny saved is a penny earned.' And he was right. This glorious, rich country offers the same opportunity to the foreigner as she offers to the American. Every man has a chance, and has a right to become an American citizen. We should take advantage of this opportunity."

I talked for about a half an hour, and judging from the applause, my lecture must have been very successful. Strangers wanted to become acquainted with me and it seemed that in their eyes I was a very important man. An editor!

CHAPTER 13

A WEEK LATER, I managed to go to New York to visit Yelena and Bandi. I had called them on the telephone from New Brunswick, so they were prepared for me to arrive. Yelena had a program all arranged for the day. I felt like remaining in New York and giving somebody else a chance to edit the paper in New Brunswick. I was thinking this thought aloud when Yelena put a stop to it by saying, "You will return, work, and learn English. Later on, you can come and stay in New York. The experience on the paper will be good for you."

She was right.

I had dinner that evening at Yelena's house. After dinner she said, "Now we are going. . . . Don't ask questions. You will see."

I thought we were going to see some new friends, but Yelena kept silent, smiling mysteriously all the while.

She called a cab, said something to the driver, and after a long ride, we stopped in front of a theatre. Yelena called my attention to the electric lights on the theatre. "Liliom" is what they spelled in sparkling, colorful lights. I could not understand what the word was doing there, in the middle of Broadway, the very center of the world. A Hungarian word. . . . Could it mean something in English. too? Then Yelena told me that we were going to see the American performance of Ferenc Molnar's play *Liliom.*

When the curtain rose, I was suddenly transported to Budapest, to the heart of the National Amusement Park, which is very near to the zoo. I would not have been surprised if I had seen Klari there, serving soda. I wanted to shout! Budapest! My darling, distant Budapest! Yes, the Hungarian policeman with the tricolored band on his sleeve; Hungarian privates walking hand in hand with little Hungarian peasant girls; girls with such names as Mari and Erzsi swinging their multilayered skirts on their hips; Julika, the peasant girl in the big shoes, desperately loving Liliom, the worthless, happy-go-lucky, devil-may-care, brutal, wisecracking bum. Mrs. Mussat, the big-mouthed, perky and haughty owner of the merry-go-round. . . . I didn't understand much English, but I knew the play very well, so I lived and suffered and laughed and cried and died with them. And in my heart I breathed the unforgettable fragrance of the acacias of the National Amusement Park.

It was a dream, a dream that took me back to Budapest.

After the performance Yelena took me backstage and introduced me to Eva Le Gallienne, Joseph Schildkraut, and Helen Westley. They were still in costume and I could not help speaking Hungarian to them, because to me they were Hungarians, from Budapest. Yelena explained to them that I was a greenhorn, and that I could not believe, after seeing them, that they did not understand my language. They were pleased with the compliment, and I was proud of being Hungarian, proud that Ferenc Molnar was a Hungarian.

We met Bandi, and then went to Yelena's place to talk a long, long time about Budapest. I felt the first poignant sting of homesickness in my heart.

I said goodbye to Bandi, for his company was going on the road and he was going with it. That was the last night the three of us spent together for a long time.

I went back to New Brunswick, but after the New York excursion it was very difficult to keep up my good spirits. I was lonesome for my friends, there among strangers.

I decided to learn English quickly so as to be able to find work in New York. I enrolled in a night school.

CHAPTER 14

LIFE WAS QUIET in New Brunswick. Nothing exciting happened for weeks and weeks, and I soon found out that New Brunswick was not so near New York as had seemed at first. I began to realize that by a slow process I had become a resident of New Brunswick. A real, regular resident, attending social affairs, theatrical performances, balls, and so forth. I was a full-fledged resident. I knew people, and I lived steadily in the same place; this, after my constant wandering and travelling.

As we worked together in the printing shop on the latest issue, the printer said to me, "I am very much satisfied with your work, and I have decided to put your name on the editorial page; and it seems that your job will be permanent. People seem to like you, and I am sure that you will make good. Your salary will be twenty dollars a week from now on."

I was elated. I thanked him for the raise and for his confidence in me.

"I am going to do my best for the paper," I told him gratefully.

I worked with renewed energy, and the first thing I did was to send copies of the paper with my name on the editorial page to my parents and Klari. They would be proud of me. Here I was, an editor at twenty. If I kept up this pace,

God only knew what I could become in America. So far as I could remember, few great men had been editors at my age.

One hot day, while walking in the Hungarian section, I went into an ice cream parlor to have a cooling drink.

A very pretty young girl was behind the counter. Without thinking, just out of habit, I said in Hungarian, "A strawberry soda, please."

With unusual grace, the girl took a glass, held it under the fountain, and filled the glass. I looked at her, and she smiled at me.

"The best strawberry soda in town," she remarked.

The sentence sounded familiar to me, and I immediately thought of Klari. I looked at the pretty, smiling girl behind the counter. How strange. . . .

Thousands and thousands of miles away from Hungary, here in America. I was drinking a strawberry soda in Hungarian again, and a beautiful girl, the proprietor's daughter, was smiling at me.

I started to talk to her. She was charming.

"I know who you are," she said, "I heard your lecture at the Kossuth Association. My father is a member. I thought your speech was fine. You have a good job editing the paper."

"What is your name?" I asked.

I was excited, and waited for an answer, as if something very important depended on it.

"Alice," she replied simply.

I left the place.

The following Saturday I decided to go to New York to see Yelena. On my way to the station I dropped in for a moment at the ice cream parlor for a drink. This was the second time I saw Alice. She looked so sweet in her white dress and white apron. Her yellow hair was flying about as she worked. I wanted to talk to her, but she had very little time for me. It was Saturday, the busiest day in the week, and she was alone.

Alice smiled as she worked. I watched her with interest, and compared the big awkward jars in Budapest to the clean, simple fountain here. In Budapest there were only three kinds of drinks, while here there were dozens. Alice worked like a magician, with quick, sure gestures. Klari had been much more deliberate.

While Alice was busy at the soda fountain, a young man came in and asked for a package of cigarettes. (Klari had kept no cigarettes at all.) The man was apparently in a hurry, and seeing that Alice was busy, started to leave the store without being served.

I was sitting next to the cigarette case, and in a moment I was behind the counter, giving the man the desired brand. The next moment, another customer asked me for an ice cream cone, which was very simple to serve. One had just to sink the spoon in the ice cream, and the result was an ice cream cone.

Alice looked at me, surprised and grateful.

"It's awfully nice of you to help me," she said. "You see, our busy days are Saturday and Sunday, and usually my father helps, but today he had other business to tend to."

I remained behind the counter. I had acquired the necessary experience in Budapest, and though it was a little different here in America, the business was the same in the long run.

I worked feverishly until midnight. We hardly talked to each other during the long hours. When we closed the store together, I asked to take her home.

"I live right here, above the store," she said.

So I had to give up that idea.

"But we can walk a little around the block," she suggested.

"We were busy today, weren't we?" she remarked by the way of starting the conversation.

"Yes, it was quite busy, but I am used to the work."

"Were you in that kind of business in Budapest?"

"No," I replied, "but I used to help out some people I know there."

"The weekdays are not so busy, I suppose," I asked.

"No, not so very busy."

"Do you sell many cigarettes?"

"No, not very many. But I must go now. I thank you again. Goodnight." She pressed my hand promisingly as we parted, smiled, and ran into the house. It was a mistake not to kiss her, I thought.

That night, when I came home, I found a letter waiting for me. It was from Klari.

"I am very lonesome for you, Paul," she wrote, "and I wonder if I will ever see you again. The distance is so great between us. It frightens me to think of it. Your friend Charley is a very nice boy. He said that I am so beautiful that forty priests should kneel before me and adore me all day. He is a strange boy. We talk a lot about you. Tell me everything about your life in America, and your work. It must be interesting to be an editor. Do you remember that once you wanted to be one for my sake? I am so lonesome for you and I am very glad that you sent your friend Charley to me. . . ."

The darling! But Charley was certainly peculiar. The idea about the kneeling priests was not so bad. Just like Charley.

They seemed to like each other very much. I wrote her a long letter immediately.

I wrote until three o'clock in the morning and awoke at noon, but it was all right, since business was not so good in the morning, and I had not missed much. Immediately after breakfast I went to Alice, and as the customers were coming steadily, I worked hard all day.

Again, we had very little time to say anything to each other, but even so I could notice that she had very lovely legs, and moved with grace and beauty. A nice girl, I thought.

Again we closed the store together, and it was then that I told her that I would like to promote a benefit performance for the paper, and asked her if she would help me.

"That would be great!" she cried. "I always wanted to go on the stage. Everybody says that I look like Mary Pickford."

She didn't, but I answered, "I should say you do! Well, you see, I have to try you out before I can promise you anything. But somehow I feel that you will be good for the part I have in mind."

We were in the store. There was only one little light burning, and she was ready to go out through the little side door. Her father was fast asleep in his room above the store.

"There is a part in the play," I explained, "when the young boy comes home for his vacation. He has a sister . . ." (I was thinking swiftly and desperately) "whom he loves very much. They are orphans and have nobody on earth but each other. The boy comes home, runs to his sister, hugs her, kisses her many times, and says, 'Darling, I'm so happy to be with you again!' But the sister turns her face away from the embrace. She seems to be angry and then she says . . . But I think we can try the first part out, right here. You see, it does not take a long time, and I can judge immediately whether you can do it or not. Let us say, then, that I am the boy, and you are the sister. I come in from here, I notice you, I open my arms like this . . . you hug me, and I . . ."

I kissed her. I forgot all about the part I was supposed to play, and she evidently did not remember her lines, either, for she stayed there in my arms, happily. It was a long time before I was convinced that she would be able to play the sister part. She was lovely. We stayed there for a long time, in the half-dark store, kissing each other, the play absolutely forgotten.

"I like you so much," she said.

"Alice, darling. . . ."

As I held her in my arms, I suddenly realized how little we had talked since we met. But somehow I did not feel, and I had never felt, like talking to her. I only wanted to embrace her and kiss her lips. She liked to be kissed, and seemed to like me. It was nearly morning when we parted. I went home, but could not sleep, I lay awake and thought:

> *I am an editor, earning twenty dollars a week. With the aid of small side jobs, and the use of my brains, that will be enough to be married on. I love Klari, I hope for her more than I do for my life. It would be wonderful to bring her to America, but it would be difficult, almost impossible, on twenty dollars a week. I have enough money to get married on, but not enough for fares and other expenses. Perhaps she will marry someone else. Who knows what is going to happen? The strangest things happen. Alice is sweet, and she is right here. Her beautiful warm lips, the perfume of her long, blond hair—how nice that she has not bobbed it—it is*

> *delicious to play with those long, luxuriant tresses. . . . No, it would not be a bad idea to marry Alice. I think she would marry me. Ah, to be married, to dream with her in the same bed, to hug her slender, firm, young body, to love her. . . . Alice. . . . I will marry her!*

I saw her face before me, and slowly she dissolved into my dreams.

Alice's father had been a blacksmith before he bought the ice cream parlor, and he had an irritating and striking resemblance to his daughter. He was a kindhearted man, and sent considerable money to his poor relatives living in Hungary.

"I just got a letter from Michael," he would say. "They received the hundred dollars I sent them through Birkas, the banker. He got fifty thousand kronen for it. That is a fortune there. Mr. Birkas is a great man."

"When did you send the money?" I inquired.

"One month ago."

I was immediately suspicious, but could not tell him exactly what the Hungarian kronen was worth a month ago. After a short investigation, I found out that Michael should have received seventy thousand kronen. Evidently Birkas was cheating. When I told Alice's father and proved it to him, he was furious.

"I am going to kill that thief!" he shouted.

Once started on this line, I began to investigate cautiously and quietly, and discovered that Birkas was constantly defrauding the poor Hungarians who sent money to Hungary through his bank. In the next issue of our paper, I published the current exchange rate of the kronen in dollars.

"I'm going to stop advertising with you if you don't stop publishing the exchange rate in the papers," Birkas told me.

"That's not a bad idea," I answered calmly. "I'm going to publish the facts about Hungarian money no matter what you do. We have to protect our readers."

My boss, the printer, was not in New Brunswick at the moment, and though I was taking a chance in doing this, I was sure he would agree with me when he returned. I had many affidavits in my hands to prove that Birkas was cheating the Hungarians.

As Birkas was about to leave the office, he turned to me and said, "Listen you. . . . I'm a good man. If I'm a friend, I'm a good one; but if you make an enemy out of me, you'll be sorry for it for the rest of your life."

"We'll see about that," I answered.

Birkas was a rich and powerful man. But I felt it was my duty to protect the people. It was a beautiful and sacred duty, and I couldn't afford to be frightened off my course. I was going through with the business. I immediately wrote a long, strongly worded article warning the Hungarians and publishing some facts about the banker's crooked business methods.

When my employer returned, and learned what had transpired in his absence, he said to me, "This was a bad move, Paul. He is a very strong and dangerous man; and I have a family. You will have to stop the campaign against him."

"But," I insisted, "can't you see that it is our duty to protect the people? We have to fight to the finish. He is a crook, a common thief."

"You are very young, my boy. I hate him myself, and have known for a long time that he was cheating the people, but he has been a good advertiser; and I know he can be a dangerous enemy. We will have to stop those articles. I have to think of my family."

But I was persistent.

"I will sign every article," I said, "I'm willing to take the responsibility alone. The people will recognize the fact that I am their true friend. I must go on with the fight."

"But I am the publisher," he demurred, "and the law will hold me responsible, unless . . ." the rest of the sentence was unspoken. He appeared to be deep in thought. After a long pause, he said abruptly, "I think I can make you the publisher of the paper until the fight is over. Then nobody can hold me responsible. Of course I will remove your name from the paper when the affair is finished."

I wanted to shout with joy. A publisher, and the savior of the people! I almost liked the crooked banker for it. I would get all the credit, and the poor victims would give me all their gratitude. Alice and her father would look up to me. I was willing to sacrifice anything for the benefit of the people. As if turning over the offer in my mind, I calmly thanked the publisher.

After that I continued writing articles against the banker, and of course sent copies of the paper to my parents and to Klari. My name was printed on the editorial page as both the editor and publisher. My articles created a big sensation among the Hungarians. Alice's father was overjoyed.

"We'll show the dirty crook!" he said over and over again.

A few weeks passed. I was the hero of New Brunswick. The banker sent his lawyer to me demanding an apology in the paper and a stop to the articles. He threatened to send me to jail. I laughed at the lawyer and said, "Tell him that I will fight to the finish. He had better leave town."

The lawyer smiled.

"We are trying to do you a favor. But if you are so stubborn, you will see what will happen."

Of course I would see. I would save the people and punish the crook! The thief! The cheat!

CHAPTER 15

One day I was handed a summons. When I appeared in court, I was put under three thousand dollars bail, for criminal libel, and taken to the police station pending further instructions.

It would be an interesting experience, I thought, for I was sure that within an hour Alice's father, the printer, and perhaps a few others would arrive with the bail.

In my small, uncomfortable, badly lit cell I tried to be brave, nonchalant. I tried to feel as if I were a hero, a martyr, sacrificing himself on the altar of justice. But I was in a cell, like any murderer, thief, or other criminal. Everything was quiet, mysterious, threatening. Who could tell what was going to happen to me? I remembered stories in which powerful enemies did horrible, cruel things to innocent people. My enemy, the banker, was powerful enough to put me in jail. Who knew what might happen to a stranger in a strange country? Two or three hours had already passed.

Perhaps they would forget about me, I thought, and for a long weary years leave me to rot in jail. In my childhood my father had frightened us by saying, "I will put you in jail," when we were naughty. It was the worst threat he could think of. And now here I was, in a real jail, in a dark, horrible cell. A lonely prisoner.

I sat there terribly depressed, thinking dark thoughts, when a big gate swung open and a policeman entered carrying a man whose face was covered with blood. He was bleeding freely from cuts on his face and hands. The newcomer was tall and heavily built. He cursed and fought, trying to free himself from the officer's grasp. The policeman lifted his club and hit the giant on the head. The cursing ceased. I heard the thud of his body as it fell to the floor. The policeman left, closing the door behind him. I was profoundly shocked.

How had I come to be here? What had happened? I suddenly realized I was really in jail. I had to get out! I had to! I hadn't done anything, honestly, I hadn't. I battered desperately at the bars, screaming hopelessly, "Please, let me out! I am innocent! Please . . . please . . . please!"

There was no answer. Everything was deathly quiet. Nobody would ever come for me. Nobody knew and nobody was interested. Nobody would ever help me. The thought weakened me. I sank down upon the bed. Suddenly I started up again. The darkness seemed to start moving around me. With bulging eyes I saw many strange, immense bugs on the wall, on the floor, everywhere. I tried to frighten them away by stamping my feet, but they were brave and refused to go. No wonder, being accustomed to murderers and other criminals. I determined to kill them, but it seemed impossible. They were too ugly, too big, and too fat. And to think that in Japan they ate bugs! *I can only die,* I thought, and with a sudden gesture I raised my foot, ready to kill one bug. It was an unusually large, crisp, hardboiled insect. The noise the execution made sickened me. I gave up the futile fight. I would rather have died than kill another one. If I were Japanese. . . . But perhaps it was only talk that they ate bugs. After my first and only killing, I spent my time dodging them. I was not a born murderer, obviously.

Finally, after I don't know how long, the door opened and a policeman came for me.

"Am I free now?" I asked.

He made no effort to answer me. To a detective who accompanied him, he said, "He is being transferred. Take him to the county jail."

The detective produced handcuffs and snapped one bracelet on my wrist and the other on his own, thus fastening us together. We stepped onto a public bus, and immediately all eyes were on my hand and the handcuffs. It was obvious that I was not the detective.

I heard the driver shift gears. I heard the bus stop and start, but otherwise I was in lethargy. I simply could not believe that the experience could possibly be real. I closed my eyes, but still I saw the picture of myself, in a strange city, in America, handcuffed like a murderer. I scarcely noticed the pain. That really did not matter. It was the humiliation that hurt; the staring strangers, and I, for no reason at all, in such a position, handcuffed!

Darling Yelena, and Bandi and Klari and my father, and everyone who is dear to me, I thought, *please try to understand. Don't hate me for this. I wanted to give justice to the people. Even now I say that the banker was crooked, and it was my duty, as a servant of the people to show, to prove it. . . .*

I was afraid to look up, for fear of seeing somebody I knew.

A lovely, frightened young girl tiptoed up to the detective and whispered, "Such a nice young boy! What is the trouble?"

"Murder," replied the detective seriously.

The girl ran back to her seat with wide-open, horror-stricken eyes.

The ride was over.

At the county jail I had to turn in my valuables, which amounted to a few dollars. Then I had to take a bath, and they gave me a coarse suit and took me downstairs to my cell. Before I could realize what had happened, the heavy door had closed behind me.

But somehow in this jail it was not so bad anymore. I was almost happy when the detective removed the handcuffs from my wrist and I was forced into activity, bathing, dressing, answering questions. No matter what might happen now, that horrible bus ride was over.

My fellow prisoners welcomed me cheerfully. They were glad to see a newcomer. That was the only diversion in the monotony of prison life. I was put into a large cell that contained ten small, cagelike cells, one for each prisoner. When I arrived all the prisoners were in their respective cages.

I was tired and worn, and could hardly stand on my feet. The excitement had exhausted me. It was very late, and all I wanted was sleep and a clear head in the morning to think over the situation. I carefully examined my cell for bugs but, not finding any, I lay on the bed and tried to sleep.

But disturbing things began to happen.

CHAPTER 16

THERE WAS A young Italian boy in the first cell who cried and screamed all night both in English and Italian. He wanted to see his mother. Other prisoners were talking or, rather, shouting to each other, and nobody paid any attention to the poor boy. In the cell next to mine was an old man. I had had a glimpse of him as I passed his door. He talked to himself continually. At intervals he would stop to chew on straws he'd picked out of his mattress. I could hear him mumbling.

"Margaret, my little angel, don't be afraid of me. I love you. I love you, do you hear? I will kill you if you don't understand. I love you and I want you, Margaret. Your skin is like velvet and your innocent little mouth is. . . ."

He stopped, and there was silence for a moment. Then he started to recite:

I love you for your velvety youth. . . .
I will serve you day and night.
I will serve you always . . . ever.
I will be your living knight.
All I want is to be loved
By your velvety youth, my dear.
Put your hands on my forehead,
So in my dreams I'll be with . . .

He stopped again, so I never found out with whom or what he wanted to be. He kept calling for Margaret, and finally he became violent and started to tear his mattress to pieces. I could hear the ripping noises, and then he fell to the floor, exhausted.

It was an extremely bad night, and I hardly slept at all. At seven in the morning all the little cell doors were opened, and a short, kind-looking man gave us our breakfast. The food I received did not look very appetizing. First I saw some sort of beverage called "coffee" but that tasted absolutely unfamiliar. There was no sugar in it. A piece of stale bread completed the breakfast. The bread had been called "white" in its youth, but by the time I received it, it was aged and sickly looking. Even the water had a strange, moldly taste.

On the first day I became acquainted with the prisoners. The Italian boy was only sixteen years old. He had broken into a candy store and taken a few chocolate bars and some packages of cigarettes. He'd been caught red-handed, and his bail was set at fifty dollars. Nobody was willing to put up that amount, so he had been locked up. He was frightened to death. This was his first run-in with the law, and he was sure he would be killed for it. He cried constantly day and night, and though he slept sometimes, he usually awakened screaming from dreams of the electric chair.

In another chair there was a Hungarian peasant, about fifty years old, by the name of Nagy. He was a short, inoffensive-looking man, who, when I asked why he was there, became very sad, and finally told me that he had thought about that very thing deeply and could not figure it out. It was all a mistake.

The old man with the long white hair and beard, in the cell next to mine, was a poet. He had been caught mistreating little children. Before my first day was over, he was removed to the insane asylum.

Fuhrman, a German, was my other immediate neighbor. He had been arrested for running a house of ill repute and selling whiskey. He thought it the greatest injustice ever done, and insisted he was not a criminal and had never done wrong in his life.

"A fellow has to get by," he said over and over again.

Soon I was friendly with nearly all the prisoners. This life was interesting, but the food made me quite sick for a few days. It was very bad indeed. All the prisoners liked me, and for one reason only: I was not a talker, but a listener. I noticed that all the inmates had the habit of pacing their cages like wild animals and, at the same time, talking, talking about their own troubles, and repeating their stories many times. Nobody cared to listen to the others' troubles. Like maniacs, they had only one story to tell, and they stuck to it. I listened to everybody.

I wanted to smoke very badly, but it was impossible to get any cigarettes. But I noticed many of my fellow prisoners smoking. I was afraid to ask questions, so I suffered. I also wanted to write letters, but I had no paper or pencil. I asked the jailer very politely for writing paper, but he discouraged me immediately.

"What do you think this is anyway, a hotel?" he asked angrily. "He wants paper!"

I apologized.

The next day a young man was brought into our cell. He called himself "Handsome Joe" and lived up to his name. He was very good-looking. There was something pleasing about him, and from the minute he entered, without election or decision he became the ruler of us all. There was a reason for it. He was an American, strong, intelligent, and clever, and he had committed the greatest crime. He had held up a bank and had killed two policemen in attempting to escape.

Since I had been in prison I had not been feeling well, and after a few days I became really ill. One morning I could not force myself to leave the bed. Every morning in the jail someone mopped up the floor and cleaned the big cage. This unpleasant job rotated from one man to another. This morning I was trying to persuade myself not to be very sick.

Joe sat down on the side of my bed and talked to me. His intelligent eyes were filled with sympathy.

"Is there anything I can do for you?" he asked.

"Well, I don't think you can get me a pillow, but that's the thing I need the most." I replied.

"We'll see about that," he stated.

Then he started to talk to me about almost everything: books, poetry . . . and was more than happy when he discovered that I had not read anything of Theodore Dreiser's, because it gave him a good opportunity to tell me all about him. I did not understand everything he said, because of his English and my illness, but his low voice lulled me to sleep.

When I awoke—I don't know how long I had been asleep—a pillow was under my head and Joe was sitting on the bed, watching me. He calmly informed me that he had stolen a pillow for me. I don't know how he did it, but there was the pillow.

I was sick for a few days, and Joe nursed me like a father. When I recovered, we had long and interesting talks together. I found out that he was twenty-eight years old and had a very rich father. He was a chemical engineer by profession, and a bandit by choice.

“My father is the biggest crook in this town.” He told me. “He buys a thing for twenty dollars, and sells the same goddamn thing for fifty. He does his crooked business within the law. They call him a respectable businessman. I am a crook, because I want to live, and I do things straight.”

“I think, Joe, that with your personality, brains and experience, you could do marvelous things within the law. You don’t have to be crooked.”

“Don’t be silly,” he answered impatiently. “I am not crooked. I do things the right way. If I want money, I don’t sell things for more than I paid for them. I go to the bank, where they money is. I tell them that I want money and that’s all.”

“But aren’t you afraid?” I asked. “I heard that you killed two policemen. You may get the chair for it.”

I shall never forget the look he gave me. He looked at me as an intelligent man would look at an idiot. For a short time he seemed overcome, then he said, slowly, “And if I get the chair, what of it? One for two. I win. Can’t you understand?”

I shook my head. I couldn’t understand.

“Well,” he explained. “I killed two men, and if they kill me for it, I’m only one, am I not?”

I had never thought of counting lives in that peculiar way, but I tried to understand. One for two . . . what a strange philosophy. But all the inmates were strange. I think they were all insane.

Joe told me that if ever it got out—and knowing my case, he was sure I would—the first thing I should do was to go to an address he gave me, and try a few good narcotics. Personally he preferred opium to all the others.

"You see, they talk so much against it, those stupid, ignorant fools, but they don't know what they are talking about. Life is sweet and short, and we ought to take as much joy out of it as possible. I have thought a good deal about life in general, but the more I think of it, the less I know. I have come to only one conclusion. We were sentenced to life for some unknown reason. Yes, life is not a gift; it is a sentence. In the jail of life we should make our existence as pleasant as possible, because no matter how great our material success may be, we are successful in a jail . . . the jail of life.

"Those damned fools," he made a wide gesture with his hand, indicating the outside world that he would never see again, "with dried-up brains. They're stupid, they're moldy; all they can talk about is morals. Live cleanly, they say; and then they forget to say why. Why should we? There is no reason for the whole thing, anyway. One has to do something to take the dullness out of life. Well, I did. I haven't lived long, but my life has been worth while. There are people who are born, and after many years they die, and nothing happens between those two occurrences. They eat, they sleep. That's all. My life has been colorful, interesting, exciting, and beautiful, and I'm not afraid to die. I really don't give a damn.

"I was twenty-one when a friend of mine told me about opium. I laughed at him. I was strong and healthy and happy. What did I care about drugs? At the time I lived with my parents and was in love with a girl. She was eighteen, and the sweetest kid that ever lived. She was clever and intelligent, and I never saw anything more beautiful in my life than Bee, when she let down her long, blond hair and looked at me with her big, wondering eyes. She loved me, too, for she was made for me, and I for her. However, my parents did not see things that way. She was poor, and my father paid her people a lot of money to take her away to Europe for a while. My parents had their own plans for me.

"When she left, the whole world slipped through my fingers. I wanted to kill myself, for it seemed so hopeless to ever find her again. My friend mentioned opium once more. I smoked one pipe and all I got out of it was a terrible headache, and a bitter taste in my mouth. I was sick.

"But he told me that that was the usual effect of the first trial, and that I should continue. He was sure I would learn to like it. I did. It put me to sleep and I had dreams; beautiful, unbelievable dreams. Do try to understand, even if it sounds silly. In regular dreams, everything is foggy, indefinite, uncertain. The things and the persons in your dreams are mixed together, and you have no reality. For instance, if you dream you have found money, you close your hand tightly, in a frantic attempt to hold it, though you know it will disappear. But the opium dream is different. You have a general feeling of well-being. Your whole body," his eyes were burning from excitement, "is so light . . . so light that you know you can fly if you want to. That is the beginning. As the dream continues, you feel everything more poignantly than in life. Just as if a veil were lifted from your brain. And you see things clearly, definitely. It is perfect . . . glorious.

"The opium brought Bee to me in my dreams. One night it sent me to Europe with her. I smelled the salty sea air; I distinctly heard the splashing of the waves, as they slapped the sides of the steamer. There was a pleasant breeze coming from the south. Bee stood next to me, and her beautiful, silken hair touched my cheek. I experienced a feeling of supreme, ecstatic happiness, one that I had never felt in all my waking life. We went to Europe together, and we saw beautiful places, always together, just the two of us. It seemed as if the whole world had died out, and we alone were left. We never tired of each other. . . . Days passed . . . months . . . and there were no quarrels, nothing unpleasant. . . .

"I lived a whole lifetime every night . . . and I have to laugh now when they want to kill me for those two stupid policemen. Why did they run after me? Why didn't they let me go? What was the reason they seemed to be so determined to get me? I didn't want to harm them. I can't understand the whole thing. I didn't intend any damage to anybody. The bank is not a somebody, the bank is a monster. I hate the bank. The bank has more money than it can use. So naturally I went there to get some, because I needed some. Well, what of it? I had to kill those damned fools. It was their own fault.

"But I don't want to talk about that. I want to tell you all about Bee, whom I have never really seen since they took her away, and about the opium that has become my sweetheart instead of her. I think I make a good bargain. Opium is happiness . . . everything. How angry it makes me when I hear people say that dope is poison, and if you get the habit you cannot get rid of it. The fact is, you can, but who the hell wants to lose the most valuable thing on earth? I insist that the first thing you do when you leave here is to find the only sweetheart: opium. Life is miserable, ugly; people are rotten . . . but opium is beautiful . . . like Bee."

CHAPTER 17

FUHRMAN, THE GERMAN, was very sad. He called me into his cell and said he wanted to talk to me. Nobody was willing to listen to his troubles, and he felt it important to pour them out to somebody.

"My lawyer has deserted me," he started. "My wife is pregnant and is expecting a baby any minute; there is not a cent in the house. My lawyer wants a hundred dollars before the trial. I will surely commit suicide. I can't live any longer. If you only knew how unlucky I have been all my life! What have I done that God should make me suffer so?"

"Is this the first time you have been in jail?" I asked.

His face reddened with anger, and his soft voice became sharp as he answered, "No, but it was not my fault. I didn't do anything. I was tipped off—it was three years ago—that Lefkovich, the wholesale grocer, had thirty thousand dollars cash in his safe. Thirty thousand!" He was shouting. "Would I not stop the life of my father for that much money?"

I saw the same flash in his eyes I had noticed before in Joe's when I asked him about the electric chair, so I decided to understand and agree with him, although I could not convince myself that any amount of money was enough to stop anybody's life.

"Certainly," I answered.

He went on.

"I told the good news to my best friend, and that very night we pulled the job. We had no trouble getting into the store, but it was hard to blow up the heavy safe. I kept on saying, 'thirty thousand, thirty thousand,' over and over to myself to make myself strong. I worked until early in the morning, and finally the safe opened. We heard a noise and hid ourselves in some barrels, and stayed there for hours until we could hear nothing more suspicious. When we came out of our hiding place, I ran to the safe to get my thirty thousand dollars. I searched every little corner of the big safe but I couldn't find a red cent. Nothing, I tell you, nothing at all! I was so mad I thought I would die. Even a laborer, a common laborer would get something for such hard work. I was so mad that I started to wreck the place. I broke up boxes and dumped barrels and crates full of stuff all over the place. I ruined everything! I even broke the windows. We left the place and nobody saw us. The next day, somehow, and I never found out how it happened, I was caught and sentenced to one year. For nothing, I tell you! I didn't take a thing from that damn place. That is what they call justice in America.

"So I don't know why God is punishing me so. I never did anything bad in my life. Yet when I want to pull some job it always turns our wrong. It's true I sold booze, but it was good, real stuff and didn't harm anybody. And I kept girls in my place, too, but what of it? It was my own business. The girls worked for me, and I treated them right. Some of them made a hundred dollars a night, and I even gave them money from winnings at cards or dice. But even in that I had bad luck. I made money, but I lost it again, and now here I am in jail, for nothing . . . and my wife will have the baby, and there isn't a red cent in the house."

I felt sorry for them. They were not bad people; there was some insane twist in their brains. Handsome Joe, Fuhrman, Nagy, and all the prisoners were just a little bit unbalanced. As one listened to them, their stories were almost convincing. The only trouble was that Handsome Joe, with his strange philosophy and his opium-crazed brain, would be executed; Fuhrman had made a terrible mess of his life; and all of them were doomed to utter failure. Poor people!

I told Joe how terrible it was to be without writing materials. He told me to give a "half" to the jailer and I could get anything.

"Take this," he said, knowing I had no money.

The word "bribe" ran through my mind, but I took a chance with the jailer.

"Will you please get me a package of cigarettes for this?" I asked him, as I handed him the "half." He took it without a word, and gave me a package of cigarettes that cost fifteen cents all over America. I thanked him humbly.

"Would you be so kind as to give me some writing paper?" As if touched by a magician's hand, the jailer was a changed man.

"Why, of course I will," he said cordially. "How much do you want? We have thousands of sheets. Why certainly."

He gave me paper and a good, sharp pencil.

Handsome Joe knew his jail.

I spent the day writing letters, including an especially long one to Yelena, to tell her what had happened to me.

Nagy interrupted me at my work. He passed my open cell door several times, and finally stopped in front of it, nervously taking big puffs at his cold, empty pipe.

"You know," he began humbly, "I have . . . I mean . . . I have a little house and . . . property, not much, but still . . . in Hungary. . . . I smoke . . . but here. . . ."

I handed him some tobacco, and he was as grateful as a hungry dog. He didn't know how to thank me. With another "half" I became friendly with the jailer, and took the liberty of asking him about Nagy. The man looked so simple, so goodhearted, grateful, humble, like a grown up, harmless child. What could he have done outside? Probably nothing, or at least nothing important. The jailer said, "He almost killed his wife, and threatened to murder his whole family."

I wanted to find out the details from Nagy himself, so I approached him:

"I heard that you had some trouble with your wife, and that is why you are here."

"Just a family matter," he answered, smoking his pipe happily. "You see," he continued, "we did not agree on certain subjects. I like to drink once in a while, and she does not like me to. I went home a little late one time, and she locked me out of the house. I am a good man; everybody who knows me can tell you that, but to be locked out of your own house, that is more than a man can stand. I broke the door in with a hatchet, because I wanted to talk to her. I told her that she couldn't do a thing like that. To lock a man out of his own house! She said, 'You were drinking again, you old beast!' Yes, that is what she said to me. I told her: 'I'm your husband, and I'm the boss of this house!' She disagreed. An argument started, but nothing serious happened. I didn't do anything to her. Of course when she did not keep her mouth shut I stepped on her neck, and I told her I would have my own way or throw all the kids through the window. Everybody can tell you I'm a very good man, but when she makes me angry I have to show her the power I have. I'm very strong. She called the police, the shameless thing, called American policeman for her own husband! And they brought me here. This is the seventh time they have taken me here on account of family matters. But now I know that I have to kill her when I leave here. In the old country those things never happened. What kind of a place is it where a husband has no right to have his way in family matters? I don't know what they want from me here. My wife is my wife, and I can have my own way with her, can't I?"

I assured him that he could. Poor man, with his family matters. He wouldn't have a chance to settle the argument with his wife, for this was his seventh offense, and he wouldn't see the sun for a few years.

CHAPTER 18

GOD BLESS THE posterity of those who invented paper, ink, railroads, and mail service, and God bless Yelena. I received a letter from her.

My darling little criminal, how can I explain to you that there is no such thing as a prison cell? For aren't you free to think of anything you want? They cannot imprison your imagination and ability to dream, and if you concentrate very, very hard, you can give such reality to your dreams that the prison cell will become a very indefinite, hazy, temporary nightmare, which cannot frighten you, since you know it is but a nightmare.

Try to understand my words, dear. I know that you are very young and inexperienced. I know that you are a greenhorn, an evergreen-horn at that, not only in America, but also in life, totally lacking in the ability to adjust yourself to the circumstances under which you live and unable to take seriously this really funny and inconceivable society of human beings; for you have a sincere soul, as sincere and primitive as the souls of children and savages; unable to understand our cheating laws and hypocritical customs. You must put this whole world outside of the radius of your imagination, otherwise you will always knock against rules and regulations.

I am sending you a book by Rabindranath Tagore, a good Hungarian translation. You can safely say that it is a prayer book, for it is. Read it carefully, read it over and over again, try to step out of the jail and into the world of the Hindu prophet. It will give you more joy, and will show you more beauty than millions of so-called free men will ever find. I am also sending you a big box of cigarettes. Give some to that stray friend of yours, who has helped you so much.

Of course it was silly of you to attack that banker, but I love you for it. Newspaper writing is not your profession; it has too many tricks and twists. You either have to be cunning or indifferent to manage it successfully. The people do not need protection, they need to be fooled. We will talk this over later when you are out. For you are not going to stay there long, so don't worry. Look at the whole thing as an experience, an adventure in which you are merely a spectator. Do not let your fellow prisoners' freak philosophies poison you, but do not despise them, either. Pity them, for they are sick.

I will write you every day, though I hope you will be out soon. I am here in New Brunswick on business, but since you have asked me not to see you, I will not attempt it. I walked around the building today, looking at every window. Never for a moment forget that nobody but you can put you in jail. And if you believe that, then you will feel that I am with you. Yelena.

I closed my eyes, for I wanted to feel her cool hand against my lips; and for the rest of the day I read the Tagore book, which soothed me miraculously. I was not desperate anymore. I did not feel the urge to scream. I was not frightened, for I was able to think of pleasant things. I received the cigarettes, too, and gave half to Handsome Joe. He was grateful, and wanted to write a letter to Yelena to thank her, but I would not let him. Yelena's hand should not touch anything that had come from a murderer.

I slept the night through and I dreamed that I was a little schoolboy in Budapest, trying to carry a basket as big as a house full of roses to Klari. I had a hard time trying to lift that basket.

The next day a guard opened my cell door and let me out.

"There is a gentleman here to see you," he said.

I went to the reception room, where I found a tall, old, very well dressed man, waiting for me.

"Reverend Wheeler," he introduced himself. "I see you are surprised to see me here. No, I have not made a mistake. I came here to help you. I received a letter from a friend of mine who asked me to look you up."

I understood immediately. Yelena, the darling, had sent that man, that minister to me, to help me. He made a good impression on me. He was tall, white-haired, around sixty, with a strong figure and a determined chin. He talked with such assurance, and radiated such a feeling of perfect faith in himself, that his presence made me feel secure.

"It is very nice of you, Reverend. If you want to help me, I . . ."

He interrupted me.

"I am a wise old man, and I know your case. You are going to do what I tell you to do, and ask few questions. If you will listen to me, I'll help you; if not, you stay in jail. Understand?"

He was a "wise old man," but he treated me as if I were a criminal, although he said he knew my case. Apparently he was not interested in anything I might say. Yelena would send a man like that.

"Reverend Wheeler, I want to get out of here. I . . ."

"Keep quiet," he interrupted. "I'll do all the talking. Wait. We must be very careful. It is an extremely serious case. You can easily be sentenced to ten years in the penitentiary for criminal libel. If you don't want to stay in jail, I repeat, don't ask unnecessary questions, wait and I will tend to your business. I'm going to get you out."

"I really don't know how to thank you for . . ." I began.

"Goodbye. I will see you again soon," he said, and left.

I wondered.

Ten years in jail! I could never stand that. I would die or go mad the first week. No, it was impossible to believe that I had perhaps ruined my life, the only one I had, in such a stupid, futile way. For a banker, or for the people . . . I did not really remember. . . . Alice? Ten years in prison! Impossible!

That day I received a forwarded letter from my father. It read, in part:

I am very happy and proud of you, my son. In a short time you have become an editor and a publisher of a paper. I wish you all the happiness and success, and I hope to see you soon, an honest and important man. Just keep up the good work, and don't write articles against that banker. You might have trouble with him. Be friendly and pleasant to everybody.

Tears came to my eyes, and I could read no more. My darling, clever father. How he knew everything! But his advice had come a little bit late. If he could have seen me, handcuffed, on that bus.

The next morning the minister visited me again.

"You will be out very soon, and then you will be in my custody," he began. "If they release you, which might happen this afternoon or tomorrow, you must not write any articles in any paper. If you do, you will be in jail again the next day. I live at 15 Franklin Street. When you are freed, you can call me up and I will tell you what to do. Goodbye."

He had gone before I could utter a word of thanks.

For the rest of the day I was terribly nervous. I could no longer listen to the tales of my fellow prisoners. I was eager to be free again. It seemed an eternity since I had been a prisoner, I had but one thought: to be free again . . . a beggar . . . an outcast . . . in Europe or in America . . . hungry, cold, miserable . . . anything, but free!

CHAPTER 19

EARLY THAT AFTERNOON I was released from jail. I signed some papers . . . they told me things, but I could not listen. All I understood was that I was free to go wherever I pleased.

When I left the building, the cold winter sun was shining. The streets were covered with snow, and people were hurrying here and there. I took a deep breath of the free, free air and almost screamed aloud from joy. My heart was filled with gratitude, and my first thought was for the kindhearted minister to whom I owed everything. I decided to go to thank him, even if I had to force him to listen.

I rang the bell at 15 Franklin Street, and it was opened by a young girl who immediately asked me in. I looked at her carefully. She was small, well-proportioned, a bit plump, and dressed in blue. She was beautiful, with black hair and big brown eyes. I smelled a sweet, fresh fragrance. The contrast between this lovely young girl and the jail I had just come from was too great. My voice almost failed me as I introduced myself.

"Oh, yes," she said with a sweet smile. "I have heard so very much about you. My father talked about you and I read your paper. I presume you are looking for my father."

"Yes, I am."

"Sorry," she said, "but I don't expect him home before dinner. But if it is very important, I can try to reach him by phone."

"Oh, please, don't trouble yourself. . . . I just came . . . I wanted to thank him for all the . . ."

"You can wait for him, if you want. I shall make some coffee, and there are some sweets. I'm sure you will like them."

Without waiting for an answer, she ran out to the kitchen to prepare things. She was very much her father's daughter.

I looked around the room. It was large and tastefully furnished. There were a few good pictures on the wall, many books, and a piano. On a table lay a closed book with a hairpin in the middle to keep the page. I looked at the title: *Three Weeks*, by Elinor Glyn.

The minister's daughter re-entered the room, carrying coffee and teacakes. As she poured coffee, I asked, "What is your name?"

"Ruth," she answered, offering me sugar.

"I know a lot about your case," she said. "I think you are marvelous. It was a brave fight that you put up against that crooked banker. My father told me all the details."

"I did my duty," I said simply, though by that time, after my sojourn in prison, I was not so sure of the cleverness of my cause.

We talked for a while, and then Ruth went to the piano and started to play. As she threw back her head a little, and as her long, graceful fingers lightly touched the keys, I thought of the opium dreams Handsome Joe had told me about. I went nearer to her, pretending to read the notes, though I did not know one from the other. She began to sing in a sweet, thin voice and my lips almost touched her hair, as I whispered, "I have to tell you how happy I am to be here near you, listening to the piano and to your voice. There is something about you, the way you talked to me from the first . . . You made me feel that we were old friends . . . and I am so happy."

She did not answer, but continued playing, and quietly humming the tune.

"You don't know what you are doing for me, Ruth," I went on. "I have just come from jail, from association with thieves and murderers . . . from dirt and insanity . . . and now . . . this quiet, clean house . . . with a beautiful girl . . . listening to the . . ."

She raised her voice a little, so I stopped talking. The whole scene was strange and dreamlike, as though I were in a theatre watching it being performed on stage. I had the same expectant feeling one has when the curtain goes up.

Ruth finished playing. She rose, held my hand, and led me to the sofa.

"You are a dear boy. Most of the time I'm all alone in the house, and I'm lonely. I feel that we will be good friends. I liked you from the first moment I saw you. Tell me about your life. Talk to me. I like to listen to you."

I looked at her. I didn't want to talk: I wanted to take her in my arms, I wanted to kiss her lips, which that moment parted in a smile. I was confused, and did not know what to say. Fortunately I noticed her photograph on the piano.

"Will you give me this picture of yourself?" I asked.

She immediately took the picture, wrote something on it, and gave it to me to read:

"To my old friend, with love . . . Ruth."

I thanked her and kissed her hand, which was "soft and velvety," as the mad poet in jail would have said. I did not release her hand, but drew her nearer to me, and as I looked into her eyes, my throat became dry, my voice horse.

"Ruth . . . Please . . . It really does not mean . . . but I must kiss you . . . if you . . ."

I put my arms around her and kissed her mouth with a long, happy kiss. She did not resist. Then I kissed her again and again. Suddenly the door opened and the minister entered. He took in the situation immediately, and became ugly and arrogant. Displaying more anger than a "wise old man" should, he said to me:

"I told you to call me up. I didn't ask you to come here. You have disobeyed me. Leave the house and never come here again."

I tried to protest but he would not allow it.

"Go! Quickly!"

"But please . . . I don't understand . . . I wanted to thank you . . . Your daughter was very kind to me . . . and you have a very nice daughter . . ." I babbled.

But the minister was stubborn. He did not listen to me.

"Go!" he almost shouted. "I don't want you to associate with my daughter in any way."

He was a rude man.

Outside the cold sobered me up a bit, and though the tension was wearing off, I couldn't blame myself. She had been so sweet. It was a satisfactory afternoon, after a fashion. But the minister had treated me as if I were a criminal. Why had he helped me? The stubborn fool! I had only wanted to be grateful and humble. What was he going to do? I wondered; but I did not care very much.

I went to the newspaper office, but the printer was not very pleased to see me.

"You made an awful mess out of this thing," he told me. "I warned you that it would be dangerous to fight with Birkas. But still you have a chance. I talked with Birkas today. He said he is willing to give you some money, the fare to leave town. He will not press charges. It is up to you now."

"I am not going, and I will not let him bribe me," I answered. "I was right from the beginning. I fought for the people who had faith in me. I cannot disappoint them. I must stay here and face the music."

"Now listen, don't be too quick. You are young yet. Life may have many things in store for you. Don't kill yourself. It would be suicide to keep on fighting. He is a rich man, with very good connections. Don't worry about the people. If you lose, nobody will help you. You will find yourself alone. People, as a rule, are not very grateful. You will be sorry eventually for not listening to me. Birkas is willing to give you a few hundred dollars. He is not anxious to have the case come to trial. You can start something with that much money. You have nothing now . . . so don't be foolish. Listen to an older man, who knows."

"I only did what I considered my duty, and I don't want to make up with that crook," I insisted stubbornly.

"All right. If you won't listen to reason, you will see. But you can't depend on me in any way. The minister who got your release from jail told me that you are not allowed to write until everything is over. Meanwhile I must have somebody in your place. You see . . ."

He went back to work, calling over his shoulder, "Goodbye, and good luck to you."

I went to see Alice.

Her father stood darkly behind the counter in the ice cream parlor. Alice was busy at the moment, and I waited until the customer left.

"Hello, Alice, how are you? It's good to see you again." I started cheerfully. But Alice was cold and indifferent. I greeted Alice's father also, but he didn't seem to be in a good mood. He just nodded his head. I did not care much.

"How did you get out?" asked Alice indifferently.

"Oh, it's a long story. I'll tell it to you some other time. Do you want me to help you a little today?"

"No, you had better not. You see . . . my father . . ."

She did not finish, because her father walked over and interrupted her.

"Listen, young man," he said, "I don't like your attitude toward my daughter. I don't like it at all. I don't like jailbirds around my decent house."

"Oh, papa, how can you talk like that?" cried Alice, but her father did not pay any attention to her.

"What are your intentions, anyway?" he went on. "I hope you're not thinking of marrying my daughter. . . .

"But father . . . My God! How . . ." Alice said, and with that, she ran up into the house, leaving me alone with the man.

"Who are you?" he continued. "A nobody, fresh from jail. You have no trade with which to support a family. You don't think I will support you, do you? I have this honest little home, I have a little business, and a little money in the bank. I don't want you to come around here anymore. We don't want your business."

For a moment I thought of talking things over with Alice, but then I gave up the idea. What was the use?

"Goodbye," I said.

I certainly was not destined to have much luck in the soft drink and ice cream business. In Budapest, according to my father, it had been a disgrace to associate with Klari. Here, Alice was above me. What a fool I'd been! I had started the whole business, the fight with Birkas; I had gone to jail on account of Alice's father; and now he called me a 'jailbird.' The printer was right. People were rotten, especially Alice's father. How stupid to fight for the people! Let them be cheated, since they liked it. Birkas was a decent man; and I was a jailbird. . . .

CHAPTER 20

I HAD SOME money left, a few cents, just enough to go to a cheap hotel for the night. In the morning I planned to start my life anew. I was not allowed to leave New Brunswick, so I had to find work there.

It was a fine feeling to go to bed free once again; I played with the idea that I could go out on the street anytime I wanted to, though I was very sleepy and it was much better to stay in the room. But the temptation to go down to the street as a free man was too alluring to resist, so I got up and went down. It was cold, but I was happy, for was I not walking of my free will, in the direction I pleased to go?!

I sang as I walked, for I was free, free as an eagle . . . a rather small eagle, but an eagle just the same. An eaglet . . . And tomorrow I would start life anew with renewed energy—as a free man!

I would go out and look for work! What kind of work? I was a newspaper writer, a Hungarian newspaperman. That was the only thing I could call my profession. But I was forbidden to write. The tool had been knocked out of my hand. My wings were clipped. An eagle with clipped wings. . . . What work should I look for? Common labor, that was all I could do. Not very hard labor at that, for it would have been a ridiculous and impossible exaggeration to call me a "husky guy."

The thought of tomorrow made me furious at first, then sad, and finally desperate. I would have to do something to keep myself alive.

How childishly and stupidly impulsive people were. By people I meant myself at that moment. In jail I craved freedom and often I had said to myself, "All I want is to leave this place, to be free again, to be able to go wherever I want, to walk as much as I feel like—and I do not care what happens to me. I shall be happy and content as long as I am free."

And here I was: free and unhappy; very, very unhappy. It was silly to walk here at night, when I could go back to a warm bed. How stupid it was to get out of bed and go for a walk! Why should I walk, since I didn't have to?

In the morning I bought breakfast with my last pennies. The situation was very bad indeed. Fortunately, I met a man whom I had known before, slightly. He was a plumber by trade and nature. He was very sad, for he had just come from the burial of his twin babies. He cried every time we talked about them, which he did quite often. I went home with him and met his wife. I asked them if they had a room for me in their house. They told me they had a room that was not used, but they had no furniture for it, so it was not fit for anybody to sleep in. I had another opinion about that. I told them I would be very happy if they let me stay, for I had just come out of jail and I had no place to go for the present.

They agreed; but later on, when it was time to go to bed, I found out not only that the room lacked furniture but also that they had no blankets to spare except the diapers they had used when the little ones were still alive.

I slept on the floor on some old rags. It was chilly. It was then that I realized how tiny babies were, for the diapers I used as blankets were just big enough to cover half my body. This situation kept me busy all night, because every so often I had to shift the diapers from my upper body to my legs, and from my legs to my upper body again.

I thought of all I had read about Christian Science and Hindu philosophies, and though I had always ridiculed them, I turned to them in desperation. I was freezing, freezing, and the night was endless. I tried to picture Yelena's apartment, with its huge open fireplace. I wanted to see flames, colorful leaping flames. I made myself listen to the crackle of the wood as it burned. Fire! Fire, I wanted. If I ever became rich, I would reestablish the lost religion of the fire worshippers! Oh, how I understand pyromaniacs! I was one of them, for in my imagination I set fire to the plumber's home, to the whole city, and the whole world. A new Nero burning a continent to warm his frozen body.

I got up in the morning tired and worn out. I tried desperately to get a job, but it seemed that nobody could use me—eagle that I was—so I lived from day to day by getting a few cents from people I used to know, and promising each one that the minute I started to work, I would pay back every single cent.

This went on for about a week, then something happened. I went to a lunchroom one evening for coffee and rolls, to eat a breakfast for dinner, and as I sat down at a table such a bad smell came to my nostrils that I could not enjoy my meal. The smell was both strong and unusual, and I would have affirmed under oath that I'd never smelled anything so bad in my whole life.

An ordinary looking young man was sitting opposite me, and I had a hunch that he was the cause of all my trouble. I turned to him very politely and said, "Pardon me, sir, but do you notice a very strange odor in the air? I can't figure out what it is, but it's pretty bad."

The stranger looked at me, apparently amused.

"Did I notice it, you said?" he said with a broad grin. "Did I? My God, it's me! It's my clothes, you see."

I was somewhat confused, but he went on as though he were very proud of the whole thing:

". . . I work in the rabbit factory."

He must be a funny man, I thought. *I never knew they made rabbits in a factory.*

"Are you kidding me?" I asked.

He made a large gesture with his hand.

"Gosh, no! You see, it's like this. First the rabbits die, then they come to our factory and we make all kinds of furs out of their skins."

Now this was interesting.

"Do you need any experience to get a job in that place?" I asked.

"Do you want to work there?"

"Well, I would like to." I replied.

"It's a very nice place," he said. "Good factory. Open shop. White people. I'll take care of you. My word goes there. Don't worry. I'll meet you in front of this restaurant tomorrow morning and I'll introduce you to the foreman. He is a good friend of mine. Be here tomorrow at seven o'clock and leave the rest to me."

In the morning I met my new friend and we went to the "rabbit factory," though I could have found the place myself, for it had a very bad smell even from a distance. I was introduced to the foreman and he put me to work immediately.

He informed me that they had broken with the old, traditional eight-hour shift. Here, one could work as many hours as one chose, because everybody got paid by the hours. Of course, he admitted, thirty cents an hour was not big pay, but with ambition and energy, one could work oneself up and make as much as thirty-five.

The work was simple and aggravating. I worked in the same room with twenty other men who came from all parts of the world. A young American sat on a high chair, looking down at us, doing nothing. Later on I found out that he was the foreman of that particular department.

He was the one who showed me what to do. We had a great pile of rabbit skins in front of us. The skins were ill-smelling, but that little thing did not seem to bother anyone. I was to take hold of a skin and rub it with some liquid. I had a big pail of it in front of me, and I could never figure out what it was.

I decided it was a cross between caster oil and something worse. It was sticky, but one could rub the rabbit skin with it. I looked around at the workers and was frightened by the unbelievable speed at which they worked. Like lightning they took the skin, rubbed it, and put it aside. It was remarkable. I pulled myself together. I had to do it, there was no way out of it. With a determined gesture I grabbed one skin, put it down flat, and after a second's hesitation I actually put my palm into the liquid. The next moment my palm was above the skin, ready for anything, when something terrible happened.

My hand, the one with the liquid on it, stopped in the air. The reason for this was an unusually grown-up bug who was just crawling out of the skin, very much alive. I had never seen such a big, evil-looking insect in all my life; and the thing was coming out, slowly and surely, with a determined air. My heart stopped beating; chills ran up and down my body, and I started to itch all over.

I looked around hopelessly, and saw a bug, very similar to mine, come out of my neighbor's rabbit skin, wiggling his little head. I looked at the man. He was a big Russian. I followed his eyes and I noticed that he too saw the thing. I waited. Not a muscle moved on his stony face. He lifted his hand, let it come down again, and the bug disappeared in the liquid. I clenched my teeth together. If he could, I could too. What could happen? I was stronger than that damn little bug. I held my breath and lifted my hand. I shut my eyes and, with a surprisingly quick movement, hit the skin. The thing disappeared. Immediately I rubbed the liquid on the skin. I looked around slowly. I was relieved. No one had noticed my hesitation.

Then I started work as fast as I could. For hours and hours I worked, until I felt that my hands and arms had died; I had a very definite feeling that someone else was doing the work, that some unknown hand was rising and sinking in the smelly rabbit skins. I had heard before, and I remembered having learned in school, about the habits of rabbits, but I had never really believed that rabbits could multiply with such aggravating and amazing rapidity. But they did, and it seemed that they would never stop. More and more skins came, in big sacks, and I gave up hope.

Night came. I was dead tired and disgusted. I could have gone home, but I had made only three dollars, and I was determined to work until my wages amounted to five dollars: for I had to give five dollars to the kindhearted plumber for the room. I was in a daze, and all I could see were big, disgusting dead bugs. Hundreds of them. I hated them with an overwhelming, active hatred. But I continued working, for I had to make five dollars. I talked to myself: "Where there is a will, there is a way. Try and try again. I must give five dollars to the kindhearted plumber. Can't I give it to him one day later? What's a day in a lifetime? Aha! You want to quit! You are yellow! The kindhearted plumber felt pity for you, but what do you care about him?"

I kept on talking to myself about the plumber and about his dead twins. Finally I succeeded in making myself feel very sorry for him, and I killed the bugs with new energy, saying: "This is for the kindhearted plumber." But in spite of the rage I worked up against the bugs—the scene would have done well as war-propaganda against them—I felt a curious feeling in my stomach, and cold beads of perspiration ran down my forehead.

"You are not going to be sick! You are not going to faint!" I told myself, with plenty of threats and curses. I had to make five dollars for the kindhearted plumber.

In my despair I thought of working in gloves, but I had to abandon this otherwise good idea, for I mentioned it to my fellow worker and he laughed out loud.

They gave us time to eat during the night, but in the first place I had no money to eat with, and in the second the smell of the dead rabbits had made me lose my appetite. I was very grateful for that, because it would have been terrible to work all night without eating if I had been hungry.

Finally morning came and I left the factory, collecting five dollars only, although I had made a few cents more. They did not want to give me all the money that was coming to me. I promised to come back in a few hours to work some more.

The factory was not very far from the plumber's house, but I was quite tired, and so it was hard to walk. I had to help my legs with my hands, but finally we—my legs and hands and all—got home, and the first thing I wanted to do was to see the kindhearted plumber to give him the money. However, I couldn't, because he and his wife were still sleeping. I fixed the alarm clock so I should be on my feet in three hours. The minute I reached the floor, I was asleep. I dreamed about bad smells in Iceland, for it was cold in my dreams, under the surprisingly small diapers. Half asleep, I thought of shifting them, putting them lower down, for my legs were pretty cold, but I did not have the energy to do so.

Not long after, the alarm clock rang and I awoke and sleepily started to wash and dress, and by that time the plumber and his wife were up too. I wanted to give them the money, but they did not want to take it, saying that I could pay when I had more money. No matter what I said, they did not want to take the five dollars. I insisted and persisted almost to the point of rudeness, but they stubbornly repeated that I could give them the five dollars when I had more money. I was furious. I wanted to give them the money—that was why I had worked all night, suffering and tortured. I hated the damn kindhearted plumber and I was sorry to have wasted so many nice thoughts on him. He certainly had not deserved them. People are ungrateful, I thought, as I walked toward the factory. My brain was foggy and my whole being was filled with a feeling of futility and emptiness.

I had been working in the factory a week when I asked the foreman to put me in some other rabbit department, for I didn't like the present place very much. And that was the truth, for in addition to the liquids, skins, smells, and bugs, we worked in a cold room and at certain intervals we had to carry the moistened skins into the steam room, which was very hot, and then to take the whole business out again and continue our work in the cold room again. My request was granted, and they put me in the "mill room."

That was not very good, either, and pretty soon I was sorry I had ever left the first, good place. The mill business was not a good one. There was a big, wet mill with rabbit skins in it. The skins were immersed in salty water, which splashed into my eyes with amazing accuracy, no matter which way I turned my head, thus preventing me from seeing anything, although my job was to watch and see when the mill wheel a skin to broughtthe surface. When it did, I was to fish out the skin with my hand and put it aside.

The fishing wasn't an easy job, either, even if I had been able to see everything clearly, for the mill went around at a certain speed, and if I were a moment late, it would run away with my hands. The foreman told me that the man who had worked there previously was in the hospital, because he'd come to work drunk and the mill had cut off his hand.

"You see, this is no place for a drunkard," he added.

No, I could not see anything, for the salty water stung my eyes, and I could not understand how anybody could work there. My legs and feet were covered with water, but I was told I could wear rubber boots if I had any. The regular workers used rubber boots, which made the work, they said, very pleasant.

The word "pleasant" made me wonder, though the time and place were not meant for wondering. *Pleasant . . . pleasure* . . . Whenever I had heard this word before, I had thoughts of a beautiful car rolling along the French Riviera; or silly, slender, perfumed, beautiful young women; or money; or power; or an exceptionally fine performance in a luxurious theatre, after a good dinner. These things were pleasant to me. But to work in rubber boots, with salty water in my eyes, in a rabbit factory: that was not my idea of pleasure at all.

I started to work, but it went very slowly, for I was frightened to death of going near the mill with my blinded eyes. Somehow lunchtime came and I still had both of my hands. During lunch I inquired of my fellow workers about the other departments, but what they told me was not at all encouraging. There were places, they told me, where one had to skin the rabbit with a sharp knife; all the workers were full of cuts, for the knife was slippery from the grease and water, and hard to handle. Besides, they used only skilled skinners, or "cutters," as they called them, and it was piecework. In the other department they smoothed the skins on a primitive machine, and all the workers there had lost their fingernails completely. For some silly reason I didn't want to lose my nails, nor did I want to work there any longer. I just gave up the idea, and after lunch I didn't go back. I went home to the kindhearted plumber, for I was ashamed to go back for the money due me. I hated myself; I didn't want to be a quitter, but no matter how hard I tried, I couldn't go on. I just could not. I didn't care what might happen, I was going to leave that job.

As I walked home, I looked into the shop windows, filled with nice things . . . fine things . . . silk shirts—those damn silk shirts that miners wore—neckties, gloves, shoes, toiletries, books. . . . Forbidden and unreachable things for me. Books! When had I bought a book last? And here there were so many books. *Sanin,* a novel by Mikhail Artsybashev. I felt

I ought to buy it; I had read it long ago, in Hungarian, so reading it in English, too, seemed to be in order. I liked that book, but I could hardly remember the details anymore. I only remembered that Sanin had told his sister, when she was in trouble, to go away, leave the city, run away from her troubles. That was a very clever thing to say. Of course one should not stick to a cursed place! Go away, run away! Why had I not thought of this before? All my troubles and sufferings were connected to this city. Why should I stay here? What kept me here? New York!

I had two and a half dollars. One dollar was my fare to New York. With the other dollar I bought a small bottle of Eau de Cologne. I ran down the street holding it in my hand.

But soon I stopped running, for fear of stumbling and dropping the bottle. Yes, things like that happen when one is so damnably low in luck. I felt that the possession of the Eau de Cologne was the first step—the magic key, so to speak—to a regular life, and I repeated over and over again Oscar Wilde's phrase: "Give me all the luxuries and you can have all the necessities."

The first thing I did when I reached home was to run the water for a bath. The bathtub was leaking and the hot water came very, very slowly. Something was wrong. So much for the plumber's repairs. They would be!

When the tub was filled, I discovered that the water was lukewarm. In fact, it was rather cold, but I took a bath and rubbed my whole body generously with Eau de Cologne. Then I packed my things and went to the station. I had to wait fifteen minutes for the train . . . the longest minutes of my life. Finally it came, I boarded it, New York–bound!

I wanted to whip the train to make it go faster. New York! My darling, big beautiful city! I was homesick for it. And Yelena would be there. Yelena! I was afraid to think much, for I expected to be met by detectives at the station. But how could they bring me back? New York was a different state. They would have to fill out papers to get me back, and that would take time. But perhaps detectives would be waiting for me at the next station, or at one of the many other stations still to be passed in New Jersey! I didn't give a damn! That was the only sensible thing to do.

"New York!" called the conductor. New York, Pennsylvania Station! No detectives there! At least none for me. Just dear old New York. I hated small towns. How could I have lived in New Brunswick such a long time? New York was the city, the only city on earth. Here one could have no bad luck. Here one didn't have to work in ugly factories with strange bugs all around; here one had a chance; here there was opportunity, unlimited opportunity, yes, that was the right expression: Unlimited Opportunity.

And this was Broadway! The only Broadway on earth! Theatres, movies, restaurants, cabarets, and millions of people strolling up and down. Happy New Yorkers! Here one could do things on a big scale. New York was not made for small people. Unlimited Opportunity. I played with the phrase, savoring every syllable.

The elevated train, with its lovely noise, with its clattering, roaring, pleasant music . . . the subway throng . . . music . . . sweet chaos. . . .

No matter where I looked, something attracted my attention, something typical of New York. How many changes, developments, new buildings, since the last time—centuries ago, it seemed—I'd been here!

New apartment houses. The rent must be high here. Seeing women wearing furs made me shiver with disgust. I had learned in the rabbit factory that all kinds of furs are made out of rabbit skins. They were colored in many different ways, and the finished effect was quite good. I was suspicious of every fur that came along. But that could not spoil my good mood.

I was near Yelena's building. Two more blocks. A few more steps and I saw it. And as soon as I did, I started to run. It was silly, but my legs were running away with me. I was like that. I would let a long time pass before writing to people who were dear to me, then all of a sudden I wrote long letters, sending them registered, airmail, and special delivery, counting the days until they reached their destination.

The maid opened the door and showed me into Yelena's room. I stopped in the doorway. There it was, her colorful, beautiful room and Yelena sitting in an armchair in a crimson robe—those indescribably lovely robes she wore at home—reading a book. She looked up and cried out my name in surprise. I wanted to take a few steps toward her, but suddenly my knees gave way under me and I just fell down at her feet, burying my head in her strong, soft, caressing hand.

"What is the matter, darling, my dear little boy, what is it?"

Then I tried to tell her everything, the jail and the dead twins' diapers, while she kept on saying, "Don't cry, dear . . . don't cry. . . ."

I did not cry. Her eyes were full of tears, and her voice, too. But when I told her about the big bugs I also started to cry, and then I cried freely, like a frightened little child.

Then she dried her eyes and went to the telephone. She was amazingly calm and composed as she called long distance and talked to the minister to explain the situation. She made him promise that he would not do anything against me. Then she called up Steve and Feri and Alexej, one after the other, asking them to come to her place that night, and asking Steve to let me stay with him for a day or two. And then I had dinner with her . . . my favorite Hungarian dishes on the table. The boys came, and we talked and talked, lightly and pleasantly. It was a feast for me, a feast of friendly words for a prodigal son.

When I went to bed in Steve's room, in a real bed, with full-size blankets, I felt as though all those horrors had happened to me long, long ago, in a half-forgotten former life.

CHAPTER 21

In the morning Steve gave me enough money to rent a room. I felt strong, my spirits soared, and I was determined to start a new and successful life, a new, fearless, happy, contented life. The first thing to do was to get a job. But what kind of a job? The first step toward getting work was to buy a newspaper and look at the advertisements in the "Help Wanted—Male" section.

As I read the ads, I discovered that there was a great demand for bricklayers, carpenters, cabinet makers, shoemakers, and almost every other kind of tradesman. But—as poor father had told me so cleverly in Budapest—I was not a plumber, nor a shoemaker nor a carpenter, and neither was I an expert bricklayer.

My eye caught the magic words:

"Experience not necessary."

My heart was filled with new hope. Experience not necessary . . . that was meant for me, for in all New York, one couldn't have found a man who could better fill that one requirement. I had no experience in any line of work except the fur business, and even for that I needed no skill.

There were barbers and tile makers; there were tailors and dentists; and these were not my trades. Mine was "experience not necessary." The ad asked for a young man, experience not necessary, that and the address, which turned out to be an ugly brick building on the outskirts of New York. It was some kind of a factory. It was very early when I arrived there, but even so, a big crowd was waiting for the foreman.

As I looked around among the people looking for work, I saw that most of them were bitter, hard, and determined. Every moment more and more men approached the factory. Although I remembered very clearly that the advertisement read "young man," those waiting impatiently and eyeing each other murderously were of all ages.

After a long, dreary wait, the foreman came out and selected a few people, dismissing the others with a quick gesture. Some of them stood around after the dismissal, hoping against all odds. I was among those who remained. When I saw that the foreman was not interested in the crowd of us any longer, I pulled myself together and ran to him, asking, "Don't you need a real, able worker?"

He looked at me with utter disgust.

"We need men here, sonny," he said and turned away.

That was all for the day. Well, I thought, the next day would be more lucky, but it wasn't. In a few days all my money was spent, and finally I reached the point where I was unable to buy breakfast; and breakfast was my only weakness. I did not mind fasting during the day, but my day was completely spoiled when I was compelled to go without eating anything in the morning. It was a bad start.

I walked aimlessly, thinking and scheming when suddenly I noticed a sign in a lunchroom window that read, "BUSBOY WANTED." The next moment I was in the restaurant, looking for the boss. He turned out to be an unusually fat man, and as he came forward to look me over, he did not have that certain encouraging look that makes life pleasant for job seekers. Behind him, at the cash register, was a large "KEEP SMILING" sign, but evidently he had never read it, for his face was set and serious.

"Any experience?" he asked curtly.

"No, no experience, but I am willing to learn."

"You won't do. I need experienced men on the job." With that, he left me and returned to the kitchen.

I pondered on the peculiarities of human beings. This man would not take a good, reliable worker willing to learn. How could one get experience if every place was like this? One must be without the slightest experience at some time or another. In the first place, one is born without the slightest knowledge of the busboy business. Later on one has to start with the same inexperience, and then slowly but surely one develops a certain degree of experience. But if one cannot start, how can one learn?

I wondered; but the fact remained that I had to have experience to get a job. However, I went further, constantly searching for a similar sign.

"I am looking for a busboy job," I frankly told the proprietor of the next place.

"Any experience?"

"Yes, a lot of experience. Not only in America, but also in Europe . . . in different countries I have been a busboy practically all my life."

This seemed to make an impression on him.

"All right," he said, "you can start now, at fifteen dollars a week. . . ."

That wasn't so bad. After all, in New York, if you really wanted to work you had a chance.

". . . and meals," he continued. "Have you had breakfast?" and not waiting for my reply, he told me to ask the counterman for something to eat. First I had to put on a white apron and soiled white cap, and then I was ready for breakfast. As I came out of the little room where I put on my uniform, I caught sight of myself in a mirror. I almost laughed aloud at the strange sight, but I caught myself in time, realizing that the funny little man in the dirty cap was myself. What a sight I was! If my father could have seen me! I hurried over to the counter, and despite the cap, which irritated me a little, I said, with the assurance and self-respect of one who earns his meals, "Ham and eggs and a cup of coffee."

The counterman looked at me with surprise, and at the sight of my serious face, he burst out laughing. Turning to his colleague, he said, "Did you get that? Ham and eggs . . . for breakfast!"

The other man laughed at the joke, too, though I could not see it. Now, ham and eggs is a typically American dish, and a breakfast dish at that. I had pronounced the words very carefully. What was the trouble, then? American people were in the habit of eating ham and eggs. My uncle had told me that American working men eat meat for breakfast. I was an American working man, but something was decidedly wrong, somewhere. Finally the boss came over to inquire about the excitement.

The counterman, still laughing, explained, "The new busboy wants ham and eggs for breakfast."

"Give me a cup of coffee and a piece of bread, and don't laugh so much," said the boss crossly.

The man served me, and I learned another thing about America. A busboy does not have ham and eggs for breakfast.

After I ate I did not stop to smoke a cigarette as I wanted to, but immediately started to work. My duties were simple. All I had to do was to remove the dirty dishes from the tables, and when there were no more to remove, to wipe up the tables with a damp, grayish rag.

It was disgusting to touch the soiled dishes, strewn with ashes and cigarette butts. Right then and there I made a pledge never to put cigarettes into dishes in restaurants. I had done it many times, not realizing how painful it might be for a stranger to clean them up. Later on I wrapped napkins around my hands, and it was easier to touch things that way. I noticed that the other busboys put their bare fingers into the glasses strangers had drank from, but try as I did, I could not make myself do the same.

When a few hours had slowly passed, the boss called me over.

"Here is fifty cents," he said, "go home and don't come around here anymore. You are too slow for me."

I could not help feeling a sense of relief as I happily left the place, and, having some ready cash, I gave up the idea of getting another job that day.

I spent the evening with Yelena. I told her that I was working, but could not tell her details as yet. When my job proved permanent, I would explain.

It's true I lied, but I did not want to disturb her with the truth. My conscience was clear, for I had tried hard enough to succeed.

Yelena . . . I could not figure it out. Why had I lied to her, and what was she to me? I was sure I could not be in love with her. I was still in love with Klari, the girl I had left in Budapest. No. Yelena, I did not love, and yet no woman had ever given me such thrills, such happiness, as Yelena. It was a peculiar sort of pleasure to be with her, to listen to her soft, assuring, pleasant voice. And sometimes she sang. She had no voice for singing, but the way she did it was pleasing and entertaining. Then her hands, those long, pale hands that had attracted me from the first, were so beautiful. And her deep, dark eyes. She was clever, too, and when I did not see her for a day or two, I had a feeling of uneasiness, as though something essential were gone, something that would never come back. She was a part of my life. I could talk to her about my silly little love affairs, as she called them, and she would smile at me. She understood without being very much interested in the particulars. She would always tell me exactly how I felt about the current girl, and no matter how I overestimated my emotions, she invariably had a few well-chosen words to put the girl in her place. It was a thrill to kiss her hand when I left her. It was a thrill to talk about things, and become enthusiastic about them with her. I think that was it: the enthusiasm. She could become excited over an idea, and yet always remain calm, clever, logical, and practical when the time came to carry it out.

The next morning, not finding anything in the "Help Wanted" column of the *World* that read, "Experience not necessary," I want out again to hunt for a busboy job. It was not an easy matter to find one. When I did succeed, I was fired almost immediately after I had eaten breakfast. Then I discovered something peculiar. The minute I was broke, with no money and no job, I became terribly hungry; but when I had money in my pocket, I had no particular desire for food. It often happened that I secured as many as several jobs a day, and was discharged from each one in turn, after having eaten my seven breakfasts.

Almost every evening I went to Yelena's, where I usually had tea or coffee, with some sort of sweets, for another breakfast. Yelena had the very bad habit of serving this sort of food instead of ham and eggs or something equally substantial. I continued to be mysterious when questioned about my job.

One morning I got a busboy job that looked quite promising. What had always killed my job was speed or, rather, my lack of it. No matter how hard I tried to please, the bosses always complained of my slowness and fired me promptly.

This time when lunchtime came, around three o'clock, I was still on the job. There were seven other boys working in the place, all good, experienced men. One of them boasted of having been a busboy for thirty years. We sat down to eat our lunch together, and we started to talk.

I found the busboys—they were called "boys," although the majority were over forty, which is no decent age for a boy—interesting and amusing. Most of them were content with life. They made as much as fifteen dollars a week and received their meals for absolutely nothing. A worn-out man with old, old shoes and bad hands was talking. He had only one eye, and kept blinking the empty eyelid constantly, which disturbed me at first. I inquired about his present situation and his life in general. He said:

"I came to America thirty years ago, after my wife left me for another man. I started to work in a steel factory. The work was not so bad, although I did not like the heat, and was always afraid that the hot steel that was flying around would hit me in the eye. Well, once I got a white hot spark in the eye." It was not so bad, because, as he assured me, "the people who get injured in that way have a job there for the rest of their lives. But I was restless and wanted to go. A friend of mine taught me this business, and I have been a busboy ever since, twenty years. You get good eats here, and money. It's a good job."

The seven tired busboys who sat around the table represented seven different nationalities. We talked about war. It was silly and futile, we all agreed. Here in America, all kinds of nationalities could live and work together without argument. They liked and respected each other. And in old, stupid Europe the people hated each other. One of the boys was a Serbian. I remembered how all Hungarians hated and still hate the Serbs, because a Serbian student called Gavrilo Princip had killed our crown prince, Archduke Franz Ferdinand. The boy was no relation or friend of Princip and had no connection to him . . . and Franz Ferdinand was a perfect stranger to me. Why should I hate him, then? We were only busboys, peacefully eating together. No hatred existed between us. We had no nationalities, but were bound by our profession.

Toward the end of our meal, during the discussion on wars, the young Serbian said, "I read, or heard somewhere, that there is only one kind of war, which has existed for ages and will exist indefinitely, and that is the war between the hungry and the well-fed."

Lunch was over. The one-eyed man rose slowly, and, gathering the dirty dishes from our table, he said, with a contented, happy smile, "How lucky we are to belong to the well-fed class. We surely have had a good meal."

With this, we all left the table. All the boys were reaching for their dishes. On their faces I could see unmistakably happy, contented smiles; the smiles of men with their stomachs full.

I continued working after lunch. I rushed around feverishly, for I wanted to keep the job. I was as quick as possible, running from one table to the other, wiping them off with the rag, removing dirty dishes, and taking them to the kitchen.

My life was reduced to a remarkable simplicity. I looked at people, the always new and hungry people who came into the restaurant. I looked at them without noticing their faces and I judged them. I liked them or disliked them based on the food they ate or, rather, to be more specific, by the number of dishes they used. I loved those who had a cup of coffee and left. That meant only a cup and saucer to take to the kitchen. I hated the rich ones who ate all kinds of things, salads, cakes, and what not, while smoking evil-smelling cigars and cigarettes, and left the butts among the remains of the meal.

I had started work at eight o'clock in the morning, and it was ten minutes to eight in the evening. I was sure that I would be allowed to come back in the morning; but at eight o'clock the manager gave me three dollars and told me not to come back. When I demanded an explanation, he informed me that I was too slow, and not worth as much as I ate.

Weeks passed, and I awoke every morning without knowing how I would get breakfast. I had odd jobs occasionally. Most of them lasted for an hour or two only before I was thrown out.

I could not pay the rent for my cheap East Side furnished room. For a few weeks my landlady had let it go and was satisfied with promises, but finally she lost patience, giving me twenty-four hours to pay or get out.

My belongings were few, but what I had I needed badly. That night I managed to stay at Yelena's very late, and it was about two in the morning when I went home. In the quiet of the night I packed my things and succeeded in leaving undetected. It was late, too late to do anything worthwhile, so I went to Pennsylvania Station and left my baggage in the checkroom. My plan was to sleep on a bench in the waiting room until morning, and then look for a job. I knew, of course, that if I did get one, I would be fired the same day, but the three dollars would enable me to get another room somewhere.

A night in Pennsylvania Station is not very restful. There is a man who walks up and down the waiting room and whose job it is to wake any "passenger" he might find sleeping. The minute my eyes closed, he would be shaking me almost roughly. His ancestors were probably executioners. He was a very cruel man.

Morning came, and I went out to look for the ever-elusive job. During my stay in New York I had learned many things. Among them was the art of camouflage. My clothes were in decidedly bad condition, yet so clever was I about the way I wore them and the way I carried myself that few would ever have suspected their real condition. I had a generally well-dressed appearance.

The New York street cleaning department's aggravating custom of sprinkling the streets gave me many bad minutes. My shoes sopped up cold water every time I crossed a street. It took me a long time to learn how to walk under the circumstances. By circumstances I mean the holes in both shoes. I had to cross streets walking on my heels. It was very comfortable and satisfying to reach the sidewalk again and put my feet down, dry.

That morning at seven o'clock I started to work in a lunchroom, and although I was terribly sleepy all day, not only did I hold the job, but in the evening the boss also told me to be back early the next morning, because if I came late, I would find my place filled.

I was overcome with joy, but found it difficult to believe I would not be fired. I needed the one day's pay very badly, for I did not have a cent in my pockets and had no place to sleep.

"Can I have today's pay?" I asked the boss.

"No," he answered, "I can't give it to you. We pay only once a week. I could give you the money, but in that case you would not come back to work tomorrow. We would have to look for somebody else."

"All right. Pay me and I quit." I was desperately in need of the three dollars.

He was strangely angered. He handed me the money, and I walked happily out of the lunchroom. I stood in the front of the place for a while until he put out the very familiar sign:

"BUSBOY WANTED."

I walked back in.

"I see that you need a good, reliable busboy. You fired a boy not so long ago on account of money. I just saw the sign outside, and here I am for the job. I have been working here all day and you seemed satisfied with my work. You aren't taking any chances by hiring me again. I needed today's pay very badly, but now that I have it, I can wait until pay day comes."

"Get the hell out of here, you . . ." he shouted, and then he restrained himself, turned, and went into the kitchen.

A strange man! If I had been in his place, I would have hired myself. However, people differ.

I went to look for a cheap, furnished room. After a long search, I noticed a very poor looking house in a very low-end section of the city. I rang the bell. A large colored woman opened the door.

"What do you want?" she asked.

"I am looking for a room," I replied.

"I have a room, but this is a colored section, and I have only colored roomers in the house."

I was tired and worn out from working all day, and the long walk had not been particularly restful. The thought of looking further made me sick.

"Is there any chance I could see the room you have?" I asked.

"Well, I told you that I have only colored people in the building, but if you want . . ."

She led the way in. After climbing several flights of moldy stairs, I found the room was in the attic. It was dark, stuffy, and had very little ventilation; but it was only two dollars a week. I took it and gave her a week's rent.

The woman seemed very pleased. She smiled.

I retrieved my suitcase from the checkroom at Pennsylvania Station and tried to make myself at home in my new quarters.

I never had enough money to even think of getting a decent job, for I wanted breakfast in the morning, and the easiest way to get it was to get a job as busboy. At that time my dream was to stay in the busboy business for a week or two, in which time I could save enough of my wages to start looking for a permanent job, a position.

But in addition to my many odd jobs and jobless days, a general feeling of apathy and indifference had come over me; an I-don't-give-a-damn feeling. I did not even have the energy to look for a job. When I was refused in the first place, instead of trying again I gave up job hunting for the day, with a sort of relief.

One day, walking aimlessly along the street, I noticed a very interesting advertisement.

"Let us furnish the money for your vacation," it said.

The ad went on to read, "Let us start you in business. If you need money for any purpose come to us; we can help you." At last I had found the place I was looking for: The Morris Plan Bank! Immediately I went into the bank and inquired how I could take out a loan. The clerk gave me a blank application form and told me to wait my turn, since others also wanted money.

After waiting a long time, I was shown into a small office.

"What is your name?" the man sitting at the desk inquired. "What do you need the money for? How much do you want?"

"I want fifty dollars," I replied, "I need it because I have no money."

"Where are you working?"

"I am not working."

"What is your business?"

"I have no business."

"How do you expect to get money, then?"

"I need money badly."

"We give money only to those who have been working in one place for more than two years, and who can get two coguarantors with good dependable incomes to sign for them," he told me.

I had to laugh.

"Why, you don't think that people who are working and who have rich coguarantors hanging around would come to you for money? How stupid!"

But he was not interested in my opinion, and he asked me to leave, as there were many people waiting.

I went, but not in a good mood. Something must be wrong with the world, I thought. They give money only to those who do not need it. They wouldn't give me money, though no one could possibly need it more badly than I. To hell with them!

The most important thing was that I actually had a room to sleep in. One could eat somewhere. If nothing else happened I could always get one of those so-called after-dinner lunches at Yelena's house, with the usual tea or coffee.

Of course there were times when I was badly disappointed with those little meals she served. One glorious Sunday I awoke very hungry, which was not surprising, since I had not eaten the previous day. I walked over to Yelena's place, which was quite a trip and only increased my appetite. When I arrived she told me she was expecting a few people, and would have a little party. I immediately brightened up, thinking of all the food she might serve. The guests arrived, and I almost wept with disappointment when she served ice cream with thin, silly looking cookies. I hated ice cream even in peacetime, and just then I was at war with hunger. However, I could do nothing but smile at the aggravating ladies and try to take big bites of the frozen cream. I did not succeed in either. I was too miserable to be pleasant, and not only was the ice cream cold but it was also of a particularly unpleasant flavor.

I hated Yelena for that ice cream. Of course the poor dear had no idea I was starving, for I had successfully fooled her into thinking I had a job. She was certain that I was working, that I had money and ate regularly, for even when she invited me to dinner, which was often, I refused. Why are starving people so proud? Yelena was my friend, though she was a woman, and the best sport that ever lived. If I had told her I was broke and down and out, she would have given me dinner regularly; she would have loaned me money, too, just as a friend should. But I never let her even suspect the sad truth of my condition. When I was rich and successful I would tell her how much I suffered with her ice cream and teas, and how many times I had walked all night when she sent me away early, because she was tired or sleepy, and how I had hated her for it.

When I realized what a failure the "party" was, I left and started to look for a job. All the restaurant owners seemed to be organized against me, for none wanted me.

Late in the night I went into a lunchroom and, although there was no sign in the window, the proprietor told me to return early the next morning for work. Now, I thought, as one of his employees I can ask him if there is any chance of getting something to eat right away: a cup of coffee and a roll would do. His sad face grew sadder as he listened to me, and he sternly told me to go away, and not come back in the morning.

I left the place and hated myself for my stupid weakness. How reckless one gets in such a situation!

CHAPTER 22

My rent had been overdue for weeks, and the negress was very insistent in her demands for money. I walked the streets for a long time that night, hoping she would be asleep by the time I reached the place.

As I walked through bright, beautiful Broadway I felt happy in spite of the terrible pain of hunger, for I saw the city's unlimited wealth; its many people walking and riding; everybody happy; everybody working, doing things. Most likely all those people ate three times a day, I thought. Possibly there were even some who, in spite of the money they had, did not eat because they wanted to lose weight. In my imagination I could see their fat hands pushing away platters with mountains of food on them, while I—I would have liked to scream from hunger.

What could be wrong with me, I asked the night. All I had to do to join the millions who worked, did things, built such cities as this, was to stand in the long line. It was not yet too late. I was only twenty-two years old; that is not a hopeless age for a man to be. I could still hope. Of course, if I were seventy and in the same circumstances, it would be different. But I was only twenty-two. Tomorrow I would start something. I still had razer blades, old ones, but I could shave with them, and I would be smooth-shaven and prosperous-looking, and could go and look for a job confidently, with an air of indifference.

As I walked along I practiced a bored expression, the only one to use when looking for a job. I doubted my ability to appear nonchalant and carefree while my stomach was held in hunger's ever tightening grip.

Suddenly I noticed a shiny silver package at my feet. Here was my reward for my good, constructive thinking! I reached down for it, and immediately knew it was some kind of food. Just at the right moment! I opened the silver paper and saw that the thing I had found was a piece of chocolate candy. Remembering ads I'd seen for chocolate, I knew that it had high food value. Somewhere, too, I remembered reading that a man could actually live a long while on chocolate. It was only candy, true enough, but if I chewed it slowly and carefully, that gnawing feeling of hunger would disappear a little; and even if it didn't, I would have had that delicious sensation of biting into something.

The candy was round, but a semicircular piece of it was missing. Somebody must have taken a bite out of it. I did not like to eat things that were already slightly used, but this was an exception. I cautiously avoided the vicinity of the missing portion. I bit into the chocolate disc. For a moment it was wonderful, and then came the great disappointment. What swindlers the candy manufacturers were!

It was peppermint, hidden under a thin covering of that glorious food, chocolate, to cheat innocent people!

Peppermint. A strong, peculiar taste; not meant to be eaten or enjoyed; a sort of medicine. Of course in candy form it could be bitten and chewed . . . and I ate the whole thing. I admit it was a relief for a moment or so, but far from being the meal in itself that those crooks advertised.

I continued to walk. It was late, but the later I came home, the better. The important thing was that the landlady should be fast asleep. Perhaps she had been to a party that evening and had eaten a lot and drunk heavy wines; then she would be asleep with a deep, sound sleep, the effect of the wine and the rich, good food.

She was asleep. I tiptoed up to my attic and tried to sleep. It was hard, for I was hungry, very hungry. I had an actual pain in my stomach, but fortunately I was also tired from the long walk, and I was soon asleep.

Suddenly I opened my eyes, and thought I was still dreaming. I thought I was having a nightmare, for my landlady, her shining teeth showing in a grin, her face covered with pimples, was sitting and smiling on the edge of the bed. I closed my eyes immediately, for the vision frightened me, and I thought it might go away.

But it did not. She caressed my head, played with my hair, and talked to me in a soft voice.

"Poor, poor pretty boy is tired . . . pretty boy is sleepy," she said, as if I were a child and not a grown man who did not pay his rent.

"I like you very much . . . and you are such a nice little boy." She went on caressing me meanwhile. "If you will be nice to me, I'll be nice to you, too."

She was wriggling her head in a very aggravating manner, and I became so frightened that I was afraid to look up. Finally I pulled myself together and started to think how I could get out of this house of horrors. I was afraid to leave the bed, for she was there. But finally I asked her to leave, and told her I would come down to talk to her when I was dressed. She asked me if she could not help me dress, because I looked so tired. I told her with a smile that trembled on my lips, that for a long time I had dressed alone, and could manage very nicely if she would leave the room.

She became angry immediately and started screaming at me.

"Well, young man, you are mistaken if you think you can take anything out of this room and this house. You owe me three weeks' rent, six dollars! How long do you think you can go on? I want my money," she gulped, "and I want it damn fast!"

I assured her I had no intention of taking any of my belongings from the room until I had paid my rent, which I would do that day. I would find the money at the post office for sure; the money I had been expecting for the last few days. It had to come a long distance, but good Lord, today was Monday, and it was absolutely due. I smiled an assuring and encouraging smile. I could pay everything. Not only that, but I would pay the next week's rent in advance!

After that, she left the room. I dressed quickly and ran out of the house. I had put two shirts on and stuffed some socks, my toothbrush, and a few other necessities into my pockets, for I did not intend to return to that place again.

I tried desperately to get a breakfast job. I had no success at all, and I walked aimlessly all day thinking and scheming; but nothing exceptionally clever came to mind. About seven in the evening I took a chance and went to Yelena's.

The apartment door was open, so I stepped inside, and while I was still in the hall I heard Yelena's laughter from the other room. Company!

I went into the room, and there was Bandi, comfortably seated in a big chair.

"My God, of all people!" I shouted.

"Oh, I'm so glad to see you, Paul, I just arrived a few minutes ago."

"Well, tell me what happened. How are you? What are you doing?"

"Everything is just great. I returned from Jersey. The company I was in broke up. I will start with another soon, though. I'll tell you all about my experiences later. How are you? What are you doing?"

"Oh I'm fine, fine! I am working now. I don't want to talk about it very much. The details are not very interesting. I hope I am going to stay right where I am, permanently."

I made signs to make him understand that I wanted to go off somewhere with him as soon as possible. He understood, winked back quickly, and in a short time he rose, saying, "I guess we had better go, now."

"Now, Bandi," I said, "before you say another word, we are going to eat. I have not eaten for two days. You are going to treat me and yourself to a marvelous dinner. Let's go to a good place. I am dying."

Bandi groaned and said, "My God! I thought you would have some money. I am dead broke myself. They kicked me out on the road, and somehow I managed to get as far as Jersey, and from there I hitchhiked to New York. I haven't got a penny, not a penny. I was just talking big in front of Yelena. I figured you were OK."

It was a sad situation.

"Where shall we go now?" Bandi asked. It was still early in the evening.

"We can look up Steve. Perhaps we can stay there for the night." I suggested.

Fortunately Steve lived very near to Yelena. We ran up to his room, and found him dressed in his tuxedo, ready to go out. He was in a hurry, as usual. I began, "Listen, Steve. . . ."

"Yes, you can stay here . . . I am not coming home tonight. I shall be with Kitty. Gee, I'm late. Goodbye, boys."

He dashed away before we had time to realize that our dinner had dashed away with him.

"Well," I said forlornly, "at least we have a place to stay for the night. The landlady will not find out that we are here. Anyway, I don't think she would mind for one night. We can get up early in the morning and sneak out. She won't be up. If she does stop us, we can say that we have just come up to see Steve."

We tried to talk, but it was hard work. We were hungry, and all we could think of was food. We decided to go to bed and get some sleep. In the morning things would clear up somehow.

After vain efforts to get to sleep, I got up, turned on the light, and looked around the room. Bandi remained hopelessly in bed. I thought perhaps I could find some long forgotten food somewhere, maybe some good, stale bread. Or perhaps there was money hidden somewhere. I started a feverish search. Steve was rather careless, but for some reason he had not left any money lying around his room. I decided to use the "square system" in my search. I covered every square inch of the room but my efforts were in vain. I hated Steve for not leaving even a dime in one of his suits. Somehow, by instinct, I left a vase to the last. It was a large vase and quite an amount of money could have been hidden inside. I pointed it out to Bandi, but he wearily turned his back and begged me to give up my fruitless quest.

I stepped on a chair and reached for the vase. I shook it. Something rattled. Could it be a dime? Or two? I fished out two collar buttons. How stupid of Steve to keep collar buttons in such a place! There was a roll of paper in in the vase, too, but I could feel that it wasn't money. It gave a crisp rustle when I touched it. It was not United States currency, but United Cigar coupons. I remembered that Steve was collecting them. I also remembered that one could exchange them for real money—real cash—but not at three in the morning.

I hid the valuable papers and started to dress. Bandi sat up in bed and stared.

"What's the matter? Have you gone crazy? Where are you going?" he asked.

I did not tell him of my discovery, for, if I failed, he would have had hopes for nothing.

"Keep quiet, you will see." I said mysteriously. "I am nervous. A little walk will do me good. All doctors agree that walking is very healthy."

Bandi said something about my being an idiot, but I paid no attention to him, and left the house as quietly as possible. Nearby I found a little restaurant that was open all night.

I went in, just as an ordinary young man would. I went to the counterman and said, "Three ham and egg sandwiches, three fried ham sandwiches, and two cups of coffee in a container, to take out, please."

The counterman's face did not register joy, sorrow, or any other emotion. He gave the order to the chef like a machine and waited. I waited also. We waited together. There were only one or two people in the restaurant. My heart beat in my throat, because I was not sure what would be the end of my adventure.

The sandwiches were ready. The time was ripe for me to act. The counterman wrapped them carefully, handed them to me, and stood there waiting for the money. I did not reach out my hand for the bag, which immediately confused the man; he sensed something in the air. I started my speech hopefully.

"Now listen, boss, I have no money, but . . ."

"Well then, beat it. This is not a . . ." he interrupted me.

"Wait a moment, wait a moment, please. I am not going to take those sandwiches unless you ask me to do so. I have a very good proposition for you. If you don't like it, I might as well leave the food here. Yes, it's true, I have no money, but I have real United Cigar Stores Incorporated coupons. You can sell them for cash in the morning, if you want to, or you can get all kinds of lovely, valuable, and useful things for them in any of their premium stores. You are a good-looking young man, and I am sure that you have a pretty sweetheart. Imagine how happy she will be if you buy her, with these certificates I am offering you, a pair of silk stockings, or perfume, or powder. Or if you don't believe in giving gifts to ladies, which is one point of view, you might as well get yourself a necktie, a shaving set, lotions, socks. Why, you can do almost anything with these certificates! These things are known all over the world. They represent value.

"Now for these sandwiches I have here one dollar and thirty cents' worth of certificates. The price of the contents of this bag is ninety cents. If you decide not to give them to me, you will be compelled to wait for another customer who will have to order the same identical things within the next ten minutes, or else you will have to throw them away. You cannot possibly sell old and cold ham and egg sandwiches. If you give me the sandwiches and the coffee, you not only make the cost price but a fat profit besides, and if you don't, you lose everything."

I could not say another word. Fate had to decide. I trembled with excitement as I watched the counterman's face. He was hesitating, half convinced. Finally he spoke.

"All right, you son of a gun, take them and give me the certificates."

I took the sandwiches. No power on earth could have taken them away from me now. But, forcing myself to be calm and nonchalant, I remained in front of the counter, waiting.

"What else do you want?" the man asked.

"Change please," I said in the most natural manner.

He did not understand.

"This cost ninety cents," I explained, "I gave you one dollar and thirty cents."

He looked at me, shook his head, but with a smile he gave me forty cents.

I ran home as fast as I could and burst into the room. Bandi, in Steve's pajamas, was walking up and down the room like a hungry, broken-hearted lion.

"Where have you been?"

"Close your eyes," I said.

He was not in a jolly mood.

"Ah, go on. . . ."

"Close your eyes," I insisted, and when he did, I let him smell the sandwiches. He turned white and grabbed my shoulder.

"Did you steal?" he almost shouted.

"No," I answered, "but Steve was collecting certificates. . . ."

He did not give me a chance to explain the details, nor did I have the desire to do so. We started to eat, taking big, healthy bites of the delicious food; and I was happy, and loved Steve, and asked God to bless all the countermen on earth, and the United Cigar Stores, immediately.

We left Steve's room very early in the morning, unnoticed by the landlady. In the excitement of the previous night I had forgotten about the change I had received from the kindhearted counterman. Bandi almost fainted when I told him the finale of my adventure, and we immediately turned in to a lunchroom for coffee and rolls.

After breakfast Bandi wanted to buy cigarettes in the restaurant. I winked at him, and we left the place. He did not understand.

"We have money for cigarettes, haven't we?" he asked, bewildered.

"Yes, but where is your gratitude? We are going to a United Cigar Store, and get some more of those marvelous certificates."

The clerk in the cigar store was typically American in appearance. His hair was gray around the temples; he was well dressed; and it was obvious that he had a regular place in which to live, perhaps a whole apartment, three meals a day, and he might even possibly have been in the habit of leaving the store to have a cup of coffee and a large coffee cake between meals.

"A very small package of Lucky Strikes, please," I asked modestly.

He gave me the cigarettes, and then said, in a pleasant but monotonous voice, "We have some very special ashtrays, a real bargain, I might say, made of bronze, unbreakable. They are only ninety-eight cents. We are offering this very special bargain for a few days only, to make friends with our customers, as it were."

He stopped, looked at me, and waited for an answer. I had a very bad habit of talking Hungarian to American people sometimes. I got a certain kick out of it, and did it on purpose to confuse them and amuse myself. I turned to the polite smiling cigar store clerk and, looking into his eyes, I said in perfectly pure Hungarian:

"You poor, poor unfortunate man. Never in all your life have you had a bad break with any of your customers, as at this moment. In addition to that, you have never offered such a silly object for sale, and you call it a bargain. Listen: I have no place to go, having been thrown out of my luxurious apartment in the colored section of this city, which cost me two dollars a week. My friend, Bandi, whom you see here, and who is a better actor than Barrymore, and younger and better looking into the bargain, has no place to go, either, unless Steve helps us again. Bandi is a nice boy. . . ."

At these words Bandi left the store, afraid of a scandal. But I continued, without a trace of a smile on my face:

"Now do you want us, you poor unfortunate man, do you want us to walk along the streets carrying this ashtray in our hands, throwing ashes into it? Do you want us to do that and shock and horrify the peaceful citizenry? What shall we do with the ashtray, which you say—and I believe you—is a bargain? Now perhaps you realize that this is the most stupid—to use a police expression—and the most futile offer ever made in the glorious history of United Cigar Stores Incorporated?"

I finished my pretty speech with an evident question mark on my face, waiting eagerly for the reply. I nearly fainted away when the clerk started to speak in his even, police voice, the clerk with his gray American hair around the temples . . . to speak to me in as perfect and pure Hungarian as my own.

"I am very sorry, but I really did not know that things were so bad for you at the moment," he said.

"Are you Hungarian?" I asked stupidly.

The clerk was smiling. I immediately recovered from the shock and said to him, "Well, now that you know everything, what about the job?"

It was his turn to be surprised.

"What job? What do you mean?"

"I mean, couldn't you help me to get a job with your company?"

My Hungarian man thought deeply.

"Yes," he said, "I think I can help you. If you will tell me your name, I can write a letter to our main office recommending you. We need good salesmen in our stores. I am manager here, you see, and my letter will help."

He immediately wrote a letter and gave it to me. The United Cigar Store certainly brought me luck. I left, after thanking the Hungarian manager a thousand times for his kindness.

Bandi was angrily waiting for me at the corner.

"You are an impossible person!" he stormed. "The idea of speaking Hungarian to that poor man! If I . . ."

"Stop! I have a job, Bandi!"

"What do you mean, a job?"

"Exactly what I say. Here is the letter, and I am going to the main office immediately."

Bandi waited for me outside, while I entered the main offices of United Cigar Stores Incorporated. A man handed me an application, and when I filled it out, he asked, "What is your address, please? We will write you a letter." He asked for my address in a definite manner, as though I might have one. After a moment's hesitation, I gave him the first address that came to my mind.

"75 East 10th Street."

He wrote down that number without the slightest suspicion.

It was a real address, but not mine; though I would receive a letter sent to me there.

CHAPTER 23

SEVENTY-FIVE EAST 10TH Street.

This was the address of a dinky little Hungarian restaurant located in a basement and patronized almost exclusively by greenhorns and Yelena. The owner was a skinny, tall, elderly Hungarian by the name of Rozsa. He was drunk most of the time. His only pride was the fact that he had once served a real baron in his inn, back in "good old Hungary." It had been at election time, and a picture had been taken. When he was drunk, Rozsa would take the picture down from the wall, dust it carefully, and proudly point out the baron and himself. Sometimes the patrons—at least those with some knowledge of the busboy and waiter business (are there any greenhorns without at least some?)—helped in the kitchen and waited on the guests. In return we had marvelous dinners for fifty cents. If one caught Rozsa at the right moment, one could owe him money, too, which was not the last attraction of the place.

Rozsa's patrons were strange. Many of them were friends of Yelena's, though not as close friends as Bandi and myself. I was not interested in them. Yelena and Bandi meant so much to me, it seemed as though I were incapable of more friendship. If I hadn't been so absorbed in them, I am sure I would have belonged to the group that spent its evening at Rozsa's place. They were boys about my age or a little older, but all in their twenties.

Alexej, who had a Russian soul and wrote beautiful Hungarian poetry, worked there as a waiter. He had been an officer in the Hungarian army. After the war and the revolutions there was nothing for him to do, for an officer cannot become a waiter in Hungary, so he had come to America with glorious dreams of becoming great. So far he was only a failure, because he could not forget he had been an officer. He carried the dishes with an officer's dignity. All his plans and dreams had resolved themselves into one: to go back to Hungary with money. He would never have money, of course, for he squandered it away as soon as he saved up any amount. With money in his pocket he became a carefree and careless officer again, visited the most elegant nightclubs, and arranged hilarious, old-fashioned, spirited Hungarian affairs, officer-style.

Then there was Frank, whom I liked best of all the group. A pale, sickly looking boy, who had had his university education cut short by the death of his brother who had helped him along while he studied. His American relatives had sent him the fare to America, and he was working in a factory for a ridiculously small wage, saving every penny to continue his studies at an American university. His ambition was to become a doctor. He had long, sensitive, animated fingers. I always imagined, as he talked about the beauty of the physician's profession, that he could heal with his fingertips. It was uncanny how he longed for a chance to cure the sick. He might have become a great physician, might have discovered very important remedies; but in the factory, he worked with tin cans, and his fingertips were all rough from the cuts.

He was studying the language, spending half his nights with books.

There was also John, a millionaire's son, now a taxi driver. His parents had lost their wealth in the upheaval following the world war; his father had shot himself, and his mother had died of a broken heart. He had come to America, the land of dreams. In Hungary he had owned a powerful roadster. Here he sat in the endless line of taxis on Broadway, making a mile an hour. He was saving his money to buy a car of his own, a roadster, to speed along the highways once more, "to speed to hell," he used to say.

There was Andres, who wanted to become an architect and who made his living by ironing cotton bloomers. And Elemer, who was to have been an opera singer, was doing all around work in a printing shop. He knew that the steam from the hot lead was killing his voice. But it was better than starving.

Ivan came to Rozsa's occasionally, and there I often met Delly, the painter, and Rita, the fantastic dancer. Delly and Rita had been living together since the first time they had met in Ivan's studio. They were the happiest couple I had ever seen.

It was at this place that I expected my letter. As I sat there, looking over the odd gathering, listening to the talk, the fanciful and complicated dreams, I couldn't help but notice that not one of them had a decent job. Not one of them saw the slightest possibility at that moment of ever reaching his goal. And yet they went on, struggling and dreaming.

Somehow, when I was with Yelena, her confidence and aloofness also gave me an air. I was even able to make observations about those people, who were in no worse situations than I by any means.

"Failures . . . failures . . ." I sighed to Yelena, of course mentally including myself also.

"Yes," Yelena answered sadly, "they are of the war generation. Their very youth has been poisoned by that cursed war. They exchanged their baby shoes for heavy soldier's boots, which led them into mud and filth and blood. War took away from their lives that period which should be a slow and gradual preparation for life. At the tenderest and most impressionable age they were compelled to kill, when their souls were only beginning to realize the sensation of living. If I had had a son when the war broke out, I would not have let him go to fight."

"Don't be childish. Yelena, what could you have done?" I asked.

"I don't know; but I am sure I would have done something, Perhaps I would have killed a few of the people who wanted to teach my son to kill. I would have had a good reason, while they compelled people to kill innocent human beings."

At one of the tables the boys were hotly discussing some engineering problem. Rozsa, slightly drunk, was travelling from one table to another, boasting loudly of his knowledge of gastronomy. Since Yelena had discovered the little inn, it had become the meeting place of the intelligent greenhorns, and the innkeeper tried his best to keep up with his customers intellectually.

Alexej came over to our table to tell us a piece of news.

"Joey has been married."

Joey, the youngest and nicest of the boys: blond, with a forlorn look in his eyes, a mother's boy type. He had lost his parents in the war. They had lived near the border, and when the invading enemy occupied their town, they had killed people indiscriminately. Alexej told us that he had married a Hungarian girl of very shady reputation, six years his senior, and in experience ages older than he.

"Impossible!" I said. "How could he have done such a thing?" I could hardly believe it.

"He was madly in love with her," Alexej explained.

"I refuse to believe that," I argued.

"I believe it readily," said Yelena. "It's so simple, almost natural."

"Natural? For a boy of Joey's type to fall in love with an unrefined, uneducated, common person?" I did not see Yelena's point of view.

"Of course it is natural. What does he know of love? . . . And for that matter, what do any of you—you of the war generation—know of love?"

And after a moment's pause, she continued, "Many of you, instead of meeting first love in a romantic blossoming garden, illuminated by the moon, or under the pink lampshade of a cozy parlor, became acquainted with love in the war. You received your first message of love from coarse, hardened, shameless, professional 'soldier comforters.' Certainly Joey could not have appreciated the sweet love of a decent girl. Oh, let's not talk about it, it makes me so sad. Have you written any poems lately, Alexej?"

"Yes. Would you like to hear them?"

"Certainly, but not here. Rozsa's lecture on gastronomy is rather boring. Let's go up to my place. Ask the boys to come too."

And we went up to Yelena's apartment; Andrew and Elemer, and John and Frank. Bandi read Alexej's poem aloud, for Bandi was an actor and could read marvelously. It was a poem about Yelena's apartment, which Alexej called the "Haven of Stray Birds."

Then we talked very quietly until about one o'clock. We sat on the pillows on the floor, drank coffee, smoked innumerable cigarettes, and dreamed distant dreams.

The beautiful evening ended, Alexej promising Yelena that he would give all the money he might save to her to keep until there was enough to buy a steamship ticket for home; we decided that we would be exceptionally nice to Joey; and Yelena promised to look for a job for Frank, one in which he would not bruise his hands, and for Elemer, one where he would not ruin his throat.

We left the apartment together and went to Union Square. There we sat until about three o'clock, praising and adoring Yelena. I found that none of us were in love with her and wondered why. Was it because she was so superior to us, treating us like children, helping and advising us? Or was she right when she said that this war generation could not love a decent girl?

CHAPTER 24

ONE EVENING BANDI and I went for a walk with Yelena. Ordinarily I hated to walk, but when I was with Yelena it was entirely different. She was a different person on the street. In her own apartment she always dressed exquisitely, in flame-colored robes or tight medieval dresses; and no matter what color her dress was, it always signified a flame: if it was white, then a white flame; if blue, a blue flame; or red, or black. Not a flame that burns, but a flame that lights. But on the street she always wore quiet colors, mostly black. Sometimes she dressed almost carelessly, as if wanting to hide her personality from strangers.

This evening we walked on the Lower East Side, through filthy streets with thousands of children; fat, sloppy women dressed in faded kimonos; and unshaven men in shirtsleeves. Italians and Jews mostly, talking their own languages. Street vendors shouted exaggerated praises of their wares, buyers bargained for one and two cent reductions in prices. Yelena called them Babel Streets. It was a chaos of strange words, shrieks, and laughter, a mixture of the smells of herring, rotting fruits, perspiring bodies, and onions.

Immigrants, I thought, struggling immigrants, like myself. Poor ones. But they were better off than I in many respects. They had jobs, stores, pushcarts; places and machines waiting for them in the morning, time clocks with cards bearing their names; a tiny square on the street on which to spread their goods; a worn sewing machine; a workbench shiny from the rubbing of their clothes. But I? I had nothing in this whole city waiting for me. No place would be left vacant if I died tomorrow, or—more likely—slept until noon. But let them have their daily herrings, furniture, pushcarts, and savings books. Let them have it all. I had friends. I had a Bandi and a Yelena, and I had Yelena's apartment, a haven. Even if I rightfully belonged in their class, or even a class lower, I could look down on them: I went slumming among them, observing them with a shake of the head; I was far above them as I walked with my arm in Yelena's.

Yelena mentioned that she would like some coffee, and suggested that we go into a cheap lunchroom. I had no money. Neither did I have United Cigar Store certificates. I knew that Bandi could not have a single penny. Who would have thought such an innocent little walk would lead to a lunchroom? To make her forget her dangerous notion, I asked her a question I knew would start a long discussion, a question I had wanted to ask Yelena for a long time.

"Tell me, Yelena, how is it that you associate with such nobodies as we, instead of spending your time with 'society'—lawyers, doctors, writers, ladies and gentlemen? How is it, for instance, that tonight you are walking on the dirtiest East Side streets with two penniless boys instead of going to the party to which you are invited, and where you would find successful, grown-up, finished people?"

"Don't you understand?" she cried. "That's just it! I don't like grown-up and finished people, as you call them. They are settled—too much. Their lives are finished, they have reached a certain position; they are doctors and lawyers and such, and they have nothing more to do. They might as well die today. They have nothing left to do tomorrow. They will remain lawyers and doctors until their last day comes. They have only a past to talk and think about. They have no dreams, no plans left, for they have reached their petty, ultimate goal. And I am not yet in the remembering age. I hate people who start every sentence with, 'Do you remember?' I want people around me who have futures, dreams, foolish and unreasonable dreams, which are so much more interesting than realities. I am not interested in how one became the greatest banker, but I am certainly interested in how one intends to become the greatest actor or financier in the world. Reality is a bird that has been clipped of its wings. It is awkward, gray, and earthbound. . . ."

I was happy over her words. They sounded like an excuse for my miserable existence and futile struggles.

"I am so glad, Yelena, that you believe in us, that you know we are going to be somebodies in spite of all the obstacles."

"I do believe that Bandi is going to be a great actor, or at least a well known and successful one."

Then Yelena turned to me, and looked at me with a sad smile in her warm eyes, as she said, "But you . . . I do not think you will ever become anything successful. I think you will remain a futile little vagabond all your life, a stray, awkward, and out of place little boy; an everlasting greenhorn; a stranger everywhere, always forgetting conventions, special duties; a sinfully sincere, primitive anarchist, too lazy to be active and too superior to take even your own life seriously. I bet you bumped against the furniture in your own home in Budapest. I know you did not want to kiss the hands of aunts you did not like. I bet you thought that all the professors in your school were childish and ridiculous."

And she squeezed my arm a little bit. I was almost sorry for Bandi, because Yelena thought he would be successful; it sounded almost like an insult.

"Well, let's go into this cafeteria," Yelena proposed suddenly.

"Oh, I hate cafeterias," I said, and Bandi helped me to lie up half a dozen reasons for my hatred. It was hard, for we really loved cafeterias.

"All right," she agreed quickly, and with a sigh of relief we walked further.

"I admire you both for coming to America instead of staying home and sinking your lives into the mediocre bank clerks' jobs that relatives would have found for you. Even if you do not succeed, at least you will have tried, and that is the main thing; that in old age you will not reproach yourself with having wasted your life away."

"But you, Yelena," Bandi ventured timidly, "you are wasting your life."

"Yes, I know it," answered Yelena without the least trace of sadness in her voice. "When I was about sixteen I said that I had but one desire: to become a newspaper writer. It was marvelous in my eyes, to be a woman and a newspaper writer. That was my dream.

"Well, here I am, a newspaper writer! And I do not think I shall ever be anything else. It is rather late to start something new. I have worked myself up in my profession, and for years I have made too comfortable a living to give it up and go back to struggling poverty. Yes, I tried once or twice. I studied dancing, but the exercises only gave me sore muscles. Somehow I had not imagined that one learned to dance through physical pain and stereotyped exercises. Then I tried my luck on the American stage. I played in a few little theatres; yes I have failed talent as an actress, I think, but I can never play successfully in English. No matter how well I know the language, it is not my language. Not that I am patriotic, for God knows it would be hard for me to decide to which country I should be patriotic; I am such an impossible mixture. I am too deeply poisoned by the beauty of the Hungarian language. Hungarian poets give me unforgettable thrills. Hungarian letters mean so much to me: love letters, mothers' letters. All the heartfelt loving words, whether from mother or lover, I have heard in Hungarian. Everyone who ever meant anything to me talked to me in Hungarian. I cannot live in English. Then you might ask why I don't go back to Hungary. Because it is not my country anymore. I went back there after the war. It had become a strange land to me. I have grown away from it."

Bandi was ready to defend Hungary.

"But don't you see, Yelena, that the war, all the revolutions . . . how much they have suffered . . ."

"Of course. I can explain all those horrible changes and forgive. Only I can't get used to them. I love America, it is my country; and I love the Hungarian language, it is my language. And that is why I live in America, and am a Hungarian newspaper writer. I make enough money. I am saving some. I shall have enough when old age comes."

"Oh, how you talk! Old age is far away from you," said Bandi, while I, too deeply impressed to say anything, remained silent.

"Yes, it is far, I am sorry to say. Mine is the worst age, between youth and age. I am not young enough to struggle, not old enough to sit back and watch. I wish I were old already. I would be so very happy. I shall be a lovely old woman, so content, so wise. I shall sit in a very comfortable armchair, with plenty of cigarettes, coffee, and good Hungarian books. My old, old friends will come to visit me, leaning heavily on their canes, and I shall have especially comfortable armchairs for them also. Then we shall talk the 'Do you remember?' language. Of course, we shall condemn modern youth, saying how different we were, and we shall also smile at it, at its hurry, struggle, and hustle, for we shall know then that everything ends in death. Oh, Paul, what a darling, funny, amusing little old fellow you will be. I shall have a good armchair for you."

She laughed, we all laughed, and Yelena, without saying a word, turned in to a lunchroom we were passing, and we could do nothing but follow her.

I looked at Bandi and Bandi looked at me. What would happen? We had no money.

Without further notice she ordered coffee and sandwiches for all of us. A terrible thought flashed through my mind. What would happen if she had no money with her? She understood the situation very quickly, and slipped a dollar bill to me under the table. My face turned crimson, and Bandi made silly noises with his spoon in his embarrassment. But Yelena laughed.

"I am sure you are squandering your money."

I did not tell her that she was mistaken, and in good spirits I accepted her lecture about saving money. I even promised her that I would be more careful from now on. Bandi choked back his laughter, but Yelena did not notice—or did she know everything, and was pretending just to save the situation?

Really, life, was so strange. It had been so hopeless just a few minutes ago even to think of eating; and now here we were, eating. After all, a hungry stomach has no heart and is incapable of finer feelings.

Soon after this I was compelled to leave Steve's apartment, where I had been sleeping. I was the only stowaway, because Bandi had left New York with a theatre company. He was in a small town, rehearsing, and he somehow got by on small loans from the other chorus boys, because, as he explained in one of his letters, the company did not pay during rehearsals.

I had several reasons for foregoing Steve's hospitality.

For one thing, it had become impossible to avoid the landlady, who had become suspicious of me. Every morning I had to get up early and go to work with Steve. To be more specific, Steve went to work, and I had to leave the house with him. I had to do that to fool the landlady and prevent her from finding me in his room all alone. Besides, if I went with Steve in the morning, we had breakfast together and he paid for it.

He was a lazy boy, that Steve, and always in a hurry. He loved to sleep and left his bed at the last possible moment. Then he was in a terrible hurry to dress and leave the house. We ran breathlessly every morning to catch the elevated train, and when we arrived downtown, we had to run again to have breakfast, and then run on to the store where he worked.

And there I was, early in the morning, with the whole day ahead of me. My hurry stopped at that point, but still it was hard to get up so wretchedly early and run my legs off every day. It had to stop, for as the landlady told Steve, "The little guy must leave the place." Since I was "the little guy," I left. With this refuge gone, I don't know how I kept myself alive while waiting for the United Cigar Store job. I had no place to go, so I used to visit the biggest and most luxurious hotels to sleep. I dressed very well, considering my circumstances, and never attracted attention upon entering a hotel lobby. I would make my way to the writing room, sit down at the nearest desk, get hold of a pen and ink and some writing paper, and begin to think, and write long, long letters. As a matter of fact I did more thinking than writing, for it was hard to sleep while writing, and easy to sleep with a pen in my fingers and my head resting on one hand, thinking, to all appearances, but sleeping, in reality. I have slept that way in the best hotels. To avoid suspicion, I even went so far as to look up with a quizzical expression when the page boy called out a name. I acted so well I almost convinced myself that there was a possibility of my being paged. One could never tell.

I figured out that although every human being needs a certain amount of sleep every day, it was superstitious to believe that one must sleep those eight or how many hours in succession. So I invented sleep "sandwiches"—a few minutes of sleep at every possible moment, sandwiched between periods of wakefulness. Yelena was unconsciously a great help to me in working out this plan.

One of the boys, a busboy by day, was writing a novel, and as soon as he finished a chapter, he rushed up to Yelena's apartment to read it to her. I was there on such evenings, and while the boy read and Yelena listened attentively, I managed to lie back on the couch, and, while pretending to listen, I slept many minutes. The monotonous sound of the reading lulled me to sleep easily, and I was so well trained that as soon as his voice stopped, I woke up immediately.

Yelena and the boy discussed the current chapter, and from her words I always gleaned enough information to join in the discussion, though I never learned what it was that he was writing about. Most of the time I yessed Yelena. She was invariably right, anyway, so I could not make any betraying blunder. Everybody who listened liked the novel very much. As for myself, I adored it, especially for its length, for it provided me with opportunities to obtain a little of the tremendous amount of sleep I owed my body.

CHAPTER 25

OH, *YES*, I thought to myself, *I could have stayed a little longer with Yelena if I hadn't spoiled everything with the ink. It was stupid; I should not have been so nervous. How many times have I stayed there until three o'clock in the morning; and just tonight, when I have no place to sleep . . . But what does it matter? It is a quarter after eleven. I shall do something tonight and start a new life tomorrow. At six o'clock I can look at the lunchroom windows, and I can start work at seven. I am sure I shall get a job. I haven't looked for jobs energetically enough. That is the truth . . . nothing but.*

And I shouldn't have dropped that tray in the lunchroom. It is so simple. All you have to do is to put your whole palm under it, and it is well that the other hand should watch, too; then nothing can happen.

Just the same, I should have gotten back the money for the ink—a big bottle, ten cents. I bought some pen pointers; fifteen cents altogether. It would be just enough for coffee and a sandwich.

No, I am not going back now. She would misunderstand. But it is not impossible. I shall think it over here, in this doorway.

I could run up breathlessly, as if I had left something very important there, and then I might mention the fifteen cents casually.

Disgusting! Yes, disgusting; but why should I buy ink for her?

Listen, Yelena, I have all the respect in the world for you, but everybody should use his own ink. Why should I supply everybody with ink? I demand my money back. Large bottle: ten cents; pen points: five cents. Ten and five are fifteen.

Damn fool that I am! As soon as I came back from the store with the ink and pen points she sent me for, she wanted to pay me back what I had spent. That was just the trouble. She should not have said it so soon. That is why I was angry and had to leave with the knightly gesture, "Oh it's only a trifle."

And I wonder what the important and urgent business was that I mentioned to her. To walk in the rain?

It serves me right. I shall be more economical next time. I should value money more than I do. It serves me right. I could ask Steve for some money, but it is too late now. It is just as well this way. Never again from anybody, ever. . . . From tomorrow on I am going to work every single day. This sort of thing must never happen again.

If I had two more pennies I could go down to the Hungarian Inn. I could find somebody there with whom I could talk things over until morning. After that I could look for a job. Yes, I can walk, too, but it is raining. Irritating, that rain. . . .

How stupid this is. New York has no fertile soil, no crop that needs rain. Why does it rain so hard? It does not matter. One can walk nicely if one pulls one's neck deep into one's overcoat collar. The water hardly leaks in at all. My shoes are full of holes, anyway, so even if it did not rain, even if the streets were just muddy, I would still feel that disgusting dampness.

I shall not ask her for the fifteen cents back under any circumstances. I shall walk toward the Hungarian Inn, and then we'll see.

Well, they certainly closed early tonight. But it doesn't matter. It is only one o'clock. I have five hours before I can look at the windows. I'll spend these five hours in constructive work, thinking. The best way to spend empty hours. . . .

Greenhorn

All right! All right! I don't want to force things. I realize that a man cannot think decently in such a rain. The hunger is bad too. It is not hunger anymore. It is a pain, an aggravating empty pain in my stomach. I don't really want to eat anything. Well, that is an exaggeration. Because two big rolls and a cup of coffee in some nice, warm place would not be exactly unpleasant.

I must not imagine any sick feeling. I have none! I feel quite well. Perhaps if I recite poetry to myself, half aloud, the time will pass more quickly.

This is really terrible. I have to walk so fast, almost run, when I have no important business. I have no business at all. This is a rotten little town, this New York. This is what they call a big city! Ridiculous! There is not a soul on the streets, and if I go a little bit slower, the policeman will come to asks questions immediately. Some city! Some country! The country of freedom! I wish I had money—five dollars, say—for then I'd be able to say what I think of it!

After all, we are free people, and who can forbid me to walk in the night. . . . I can walk if I want to. It is two o'clock.

Never, never again. This will happen never again. I am going to work this morning, even though they'll kick me out in the evening, because I am pretty tired already and will be slow again. Well, it doesn't matter. Even so, I can make two and a half or perhaps three dollars. I can take a room, go to sleep and then work, work, every single day.

I am going to buy shoes, too—later on, and from fifteen dollars one can easily save five. I shall do that until I have fifty dollars saved up, and then I can leave the lunchrooms for good and look for some decent job, some position.

I only wish I could get through this night. At Pennsylvania Station it will be an easy matter to wash up. How clever of me to save my comb and toothbrush from my suitcase. The landlady was quite nasty, true, but on the other hand, she wanted her rent!

Just cough, my boy, just cough! I really don't need anything else on earth, just that you should get sick on my hands! No, no, this is no sickness, just hunger. That is the cause of the dizziness. My eyes are burning because of sleepiness. Of course this rain is not to my advantage, either, but it will be easy to wait for morning and then a new life will begin.

I am going to buy six shirts, too. Please leave me alone about that damned ink! To talk so much about a rotten fifteen cents!

I can't stand it any longer!

After all, it is not a crime if I sit down nicely and peacefully in this doorway. If the policeman comes, I shall pretend to be fixing my shoelaces. Not only that, but I shall even . . . even what? Oh yes, I shall even shout at him: "Hello officer!" He mustn't get the idea that I have any reason to be afraid of him. I am not a criminal.

No, you should not lie down, my boy. You shall not! Somebody might misunderstand it.

A few hours yet, and the lunchrooms will open. I'll go down to Pennsylvania Station. I'll wash myself. Everything takes time.

No, not really . . . but it's all right this way. To be exact, this is not what people call lying down. It would take ill-will and exaggeration to call it that. This is, to be sure, not more than one elbow down, a little bit of lying-living in the doorway. This has no meaning yet.

The view is very interesting from here. Even the raindrops fall nicely and rosily on the fertile earth. I can lie and stretch myself comfortably. There is no danger of catching cold. My whole body is hot, like fire.

Oh New York, you big, stupid city, how I despise you and how I look down upon you! How ashamed you will be when I tell you—yes, tell you people, who are lying in warm beds, after good dinners—that you let me lie here on this cold and muddy stone, alone, hungry and miserable; though I may be worth more than the tired businessman or the engineer, the lawyer, or anybody.

For all of you I could die here if I did not possess unlimited endurance and energy. And, yes, I am going to stay on this stone. Tomorrow I am going to start a new life, and I shall tell everybody that I did not ask for the money back for the ink . . . and you have to hold the tray tightly and cleverly, and then nothing will fall from it, because there are liquids and solid things, and there are beverages . . . and if I wanted to I could get up at any moment . . . but it is not urgent. . . . The policeman can come . . . it will be in vain . . . I'll explain to him that the lunchrooms open only at six o'clock. He, as an officer, ought to know that. What is your number, please? I am a newspaperman. I will report you to the officials. You ought to be ashamed of yourself. . . .

I could get up, no doubt about it. . . . I'm just pretending this weakness.

Dawn. Workingmen passing by. Many people. The street came alive. A good-looking young girl came straight toward me. Her boyfriend looked at me. I closed my eyes a little. I felt the boy kick me, and I heard the voice of the girl above me. She had a nice voice.

"It's a shame that such a young man should lie on the street, drunk."

They went away. Others came. Some of them kicked me. Some of them looked at me to see if I were alive. Finally a man said that he would call an ambulance. What was all this? What had happened to me?

A big car from Bellevue Hospital arrived and I let myself go, although I had a feeling that I could get up any moment if I wanted to. I simply lacked ambition to do anything.

A big crowd stood around the car. The doctor asked me something. I could not understand him, so I kept quiet. Two men came near me. A terrible fear held me in its grips. I opened my mouth to shriek, but I made no sound. I tried to defend myself, but I could not move.

I could see a big, shining disc above my head, whirling, whirling. . . .

A nice large room. Cleanliness everywhere. Silence, now and then broken by the sound of someone coughing. Everybody was whispering. The silence made me nervous. I felt I must tell the nurse that they should stop the silence.

There was a blackboard above my head, figures written on it with chalk, and the word:

"Pneumonia."

CHAPTER 26

LATER, A PRETTY young nurse came to my bed.

"Is there anybody we can notify?" she asked.

"No, I have nobody in America. . . . Thanks."

I hoped to God nobody would find out. When it was all over I would go out to work, and after a while, well-dressed, and with a bankbook, I would go to Yelena and laughingly tell her what had happened. But nobody must know about it at present.

With a bankbook, rich . . . no, no Japanese servants . . . that would be ostentatious. Just two maids, clean young girls to look after my things; a chauffeur, a gardener, and a sound, peaceful life. To get rich is not impossible. A little brains, and above all, willpower. . . . Later on, when I had more time, I would figure out the whole proposition for myself. Then a villa at Lake Garda, though of course the location was not so important—it could be almost anywhere in Italy, or Hungary for that matter.

"How do you do?" a soft voice said, "I hope you feel better."

The voice was familiar. I felt dizzy, and the whole world started to spin before my eyes. How terrible! Her voice! Yelena's voice! How had she found me so quickly? Slowly, cautiously I looked up. A young girl was sitting on the edge of my bed. She did not look anything like Yelena; there was not even the slightest resemblance. She was a stranger, a perfect stranger. I answered with relief.

"Fine, thank you."

"The doctor says you will be well soon," she said.

"Who are you?"

"Oh, never mind, it isn't important, really. I am a dancer in a Broadway cabaret, and I come to visit the poor old man lying next to you. I thought you would not mind if I were to talk to you. The nurse told me that you have had no visitors since you have been here. Where is your mother?

I could not keep the tears from my eyes. *Oh, my mother, my darling, sweet, good, beautiful mother! If you could only see me now: in bed, in a public hospital, underfed, and with pneumonia, because I was a bum with no place to sleep. I hope that your heart does not know my degradation. Mother, how I yearn for your arms!*

I felt a cool, soft hand caressing my forehead.

"My mother is in Europe—Hungary—far from here," I managed to say.

"Oh, little boy, you must not feel badly about it. You will be strong, happy, and healthy soon. You can go back to your mother. Why, you are not even sick now. You just have to stay here for a short time, to become strong."

She talked, and it was good to listen and to feel her soothing hand on my forehead.

After that she came every day and I waited for her impatiently. She never failed to stop for a while as she passed my bed.

The old man whom she visited died one day, but she came to see me just the same, bringing little things for me now. Flowers; preserved fruits; little cakes; Eau de Cologne, with which she bathed my face; art magazines; and a book of funny jingles. Once she brought me a Russian book, thinking it was Hungarian. I never told her that it was not written in my language. I pretended to read it, and praised the book, even making up a story that I told her when she asked me what the book was about. She liked the story.

Madge, the dancer, was the only relief in the monotony of hospital life. There were ten other occupants of my ward, and I was stuck with the similarity between the jail and the ward; for here, like there, everyone was eager to talk about his own case, discussing his own particular sickness with pride; using medical words picked up from the doctors, and telling all the details as though his sickness were the most important thing in the world, as probably it was—for the patient.

Madge and I became great friends. We talked for hours about ourselves and others. I told her of the daily happenings in the ward, and she laughed and cried. She enveloped me in a sort of broad, motherly, understanding love. I was afraid to face the day when I would have to leave the hospital to start the fight again, to hunt for the everlasting sign: "Busboy wanted."

Day after day my condition improved frighteningly, and then one day Madge came to the hospital, and had a long conversation with the doctor before she came to my bedside.

"Listen, Paul," she said, when they had finished their conference, "the doctor has just told me that you are strong enough to leave the hospital. You cannot start working yet, so I thought I would take you to my place until you fully recover."

"Oh, Madge," I answered, "it is awfully nice of you . . . you are the sweetest girl that ever lived, but how can I accept this from you? I really cannot."

Her face saddened.

"I thought we were friends," she murmured.

"Yes, I know, but why should you . . . Madge dear, I don't know. . . ."

"Oh, don't be a child. I like you and I can help you for a few days. It would be nice to have somebody to care for. I am lonely and I like you, you know. You are not a stranger, you are my friend."

After all, I had no place to go, and she was a dear, so I agreed.

She lived alone in a small, furnished apartment. It was the oddest place I had ever seen. It was furnished with standard furniture, but the whole place was strewn and littered and jammed full of things expressive of Madge's personality. Ribbons, artificial flowers, little bric-a-brac. She had forty-two stone monkeys, with different facial expressions, cheap little things—her cabala. It was a clean place, but topsy-turvy. There were decks of cards, to play solitaire; fortune-telling cards she consulted every day, and games galore. There were inscribed photographs pinned to the walls; newspaper clippings from small provincial papers; souvenir flags from different cities, with signatures on them; extremely long cigarette holders' fancy cigarette cases, some of them with risqué pictures inside; and cheap novelty jewelry. It was a regular junk shop. The air was always heavy with intense perfumes and incense. Poor Madge, she had such a strong passion for colorful trash that she decorated her life with it.

For days and days I lay on the couch, doing nothing, waiting for Madge to come home. And she always came singing happily. She would throw her hat into the corner, and unwrap the packages she had bought. Cakes and fruits, and sandwiches and some little present for me. Sometimes she bought colored perfumed cigarettes, or a trick box, or a chirping and jumping mechanical bird. And her eyes at these times were filled with laughter and happiness.

The situation was strange. Madge was a darling, good, beautiful girl, a good friend. We never talked of love. We lived together like two boys. Her spirit, the way she helped me, was boyish and comradely.

One very cold day, I spent the hours looking through the window at the hurrying, rushing people outside. Everybody had some aim; a place to go, a job, money. I was a little nervous.

When Madge came home, cheeks rosy from the cold wind, she flung her hat into the corner as usual, and without taking off her coat, she came over to me and kissed me with a quick, motherly kiss. Then she started to chatter as usual.

"How are you, little boy? Lonesome for me, weren't you? I think I'll get a better job soon . . . not definite yet, but I have great hopes."

She made tea, and we smoked cigarettes together.

"Madge, dear," I started, "you are so sweet to me. I cannot tell you how grateful I am, but now I am healthy and strong. Tomorrow I am going away."

She looked stricken.

"No, you are not," she said softly.

I held her hand. It trembled in mine. I kissed her mouth for the first time since I had known her and my head slipped to her breast and stayed there.

I did not go away.

The days passed. The feeling we had was almost happiness. But I knew I would have to leave. Madge was sweet, but my thoughts were with Yelena again, and Klari, my first love. Happiness—a word with no meaning at all, I thought. The world was amusing, but everyone knew its futility and the hopelessness of trying to get anywhere. It seemed to me that happiness, that rare toy, always slipped through my unhandy fingers.

Again I bade Madge goodbye, and, though she insisted that I could not mean it, she knew I would go. I kissed her and left the apartment. Outside on the street, as I put my hands into my coat pocket, I felt something there. A five dollar bill. Madge! I turned back immediately and started to run. I could not take it! But unconsciously I slowed down, as the thought came to my mind that perhaps she would be hurt if I brought the money back; and I did not want to hurt her. Then, too, how badly I needed the money! I could actually start a life with it. A furnished room, and food for a few days. Later, from my first earnings I would give the money back to her with the biggest bunch of roses she had ever seen, the darling.

I was determined to find a job. I bought a newspaper and found an ad that interested me. An elevator boy was wanted in an apartment house on Riverside Drive.

When I arrived there, many people were also waiting for the job. They were standing in line. I had little hope of success against such competition, but I also waited until the manager came.

He selected me from the crowd, because he happened to have only a small uniform. I did not have time to enjoy my good fortune, for the janitor put me to work immediately. He taught me how to run the elevator, and I became an expert in no time at all. It was my duty to run the servants' and tradespeople's lift.

Work started at six o'clock in the morning, when I had to take up the milkman and the iceman, and bring down the garbage pails from the various apartments. Only rich people lived in that marvelous house, and even their garbage wasn't so very bad. After all, I told myself, there was no dirt on earth, if you came to think about it, because everything I took away in garbage form had been, the day before, valuable and worthwhile.

I had no worries about food, because the servant girls gave plenty of good food and coffee to all the elevator boys. When I asked a handsome French-American boy who ran the elevator next to mine about his life, he said, "I am very happy. There's plenty of work, plenty of food, and fifteen dollars a week. It's grand."

The apartment house on Riverside Drive was a beautiful place. Luxury laughed triumphantly from the enormous marble halls, and now and then I saw a few of the richly dressed occupants of this fairyland, though it was my duty to take up and down only the servants, chauffeurs, and tradespeople.

The first week passed, and I still had the job. I received my wages—fifteen dollars in cash—and was told to come back to work just the same. Evidently they were satisfied with me.

I was through at six o'clock in the evening. After work I went to see Madge to return the five dollars she had given me when I left her.

I found that Madge had left the house, and nobody knew where she had moved. I tried to find her at the cabaret where she had worked, but they told me she was on the road. I was very sorry. Dear Madge, she was a trouper, and a good one. I never saw her again.

CHAPTER 27

THAT EVENING I went to Rozsa's place for dinner, and found a letter from the United Cigar Stores waiting for me. I was to go up to the main office to see a certain gentleman about my job. It seemed that my days in the elevator business were numbered. I was glad, because in spite of all my enthusiasm and ambition, I could not see much future in running an elevator. It is hard to advance, as one is always advised to do, in that particular line of work. I thought of having my own elevator, but immediately realized how stupid and silly the idea was.

I had just finished my dinner when Bandi entered the restaurant.

"My God, what has happened?" I shouted. "I thought you were out of town, working with a company!"

"Well, I was, but they let me go, and I just arrived a few minutes ago. How are things with you?"

"I am getting jobs in wholesale lots. I have one right now, but jobs just keep on coming to me these days. I just received a letter from the United Stores."

"Have you any money?" Bandi inquired.

"Yes, today was payday."

From the enthusiasm with which he ordered dinner, I was sure that he was broke. But I found out that I was wrong.

He had four dollars, but was saving it to rent a furnished room.

While he was eating, I told him everything that had happened to me. We decided to keep my room; Bandi would move there with me immediately.

Yelena's favorite flowers were mimosas, the most expensive of all the flowers in New York City. It was just like her to love such a flower, but we could do nothing about it.

We wanted to make her a lovely gift, and we had to go to a great many florists in search of the rare blooms. When we found one, finally, we were told that for ten dollars we could get quite a nice bouquet.

Bandi suggested that we should add a few roses, but I did not like the idea. It should be only mimosas; anybody could give her roses. We bought the flowers, and really it was a lovely bouquet. Yelena had excellent taste. We put a one-dollar bill—the dollar we owed her from the coffee and sandwiches at the lunchroom—in the middle of the bouquet, and in the evening we went up to her apartment. She was very happy about the mimosa.

"I can't tell you how much I love the flowers," she said. "But what makes me so happy is the fact that the flowers are from you. They represent prosperity."

The buying of the bouquet had left us practically penniless, but of course we did not mention that.

In the morning, I did not go back to the Riverside apartment, but instead I went up to the office of the United Cigar Stores. I got the job.

I was given a red book and told that I should study it. In it I would find all the duties of a United Cigar Store clerk, and it would be a great and valuable help to me.

I was also told to start work the next day at seven o'clock in the morning. My wages would be twenty dollars a week. Of course that was only to start with; later on, who could tell? There were unlimited possibilities.

Bandi was waiting for me downstairs and I told him the good news immediately. Surely great things were in store for me in the coming year, I thought happily. Yes, prosperity must be on the way. I began studying the little red book immediately.

In the morning I reported for work at one of the United Stores, at 42nd Street and First Avenue.

The manager was a lovely old man who told me all about my work, and gave me a five dollar loan when I explained my financial situation to him. He said I was allowed to make mistakes for two weeks, for the prices were hard to learn.

I was ambitious and wanted to show him my worth. I was determined to make good, and I learned all the prices my first day in the store and that night at home.

On the second day I knew everything a customer could think of, but to make sure, I continued studying all day and all evening. By that time I knew every price by heart. It was impossible for me to make a mistake.

On the third day I told the manager that I knew all the prices and all the articles we had in the store. He smiled.

"It is impossible to learn everything in such a short time," he said.

I insisted. Still smiling, just to please me, he started to ask me the prices of the various cigarettes, playing cards, chips, books, tobaccos, pipes, and so on.

At the end of the examination, he was more than surprised.

"Why, that's just great," he exclaimed. "Tomorrow morning you can open the store and work alone. I will be with you in the afternoon. A very good report will be sent in regarding you."

I was delighted. This was the way to work! Now I would show them. Working for the United Cigar Stores, one had a chance to get ahead. If I kept up the good work, in a short time I would get more money, and later on I might be a manager, district manager, and God only knew what else! Hadn't the man at the head office told me of the unlimited possibilities? And it was a clean job. All I had to do was to sell things to people and give them certificates. I was very sorry for those ignorant people who did not take the coupons. They did not realize the value they represented.

The second week the manager told me that I was to get a two-dollar raise; from then on my wages would be twenty-two dollars. It was easy to save money from that amount. Life suddenly appeared beautiful; I was on the road to success.

A few weeks passed, and it seemed as though my position were permanent. I was very careful about getting up in the morning. I opened the store every day at seven o'clock sharp. Reliability is very important in business, I knew.

One night I met Alexej at Rozsa's restaurant. He seemed to be very happy. He laughed and joked, which was surprising, for he was a very serious man by nature. The reason was obvious, however, for everybody knew that he had fallen desperately in love with a Hungarian girl, and planned to marry as soon as he would have a little money to start things with.

As soon as he saw Bandi and me, he came over to our table and said, "Great news, children, I have it!"

"Have what?" I asked.

"The motion picture. HUNGARY IN FLAMES. It's great. My uncle sent it to me. We shall be rich. We shall have money; and I'll get married!"

"It isn't very clear to me," I said. "What are you talking about, anyway?"

"I am telling you. My God, don't you understand? My uncle is in the film booking business in Hungary, and sent me the picture. It is a sort of newsreel about Hungary. Pictures taken during the revolution, communism, and finally during the Horthy regime. It is very valuable. My plan is to travel through America, stopping at places where there are Hungarians, and show them the film. I need a few people to help me. Frank and John are going with me. I thought perhaps you and Bandi might join us, too."

"How? Where? What are we supposed to do?" I was very much interested.

"I have figured out everything. I have a hundred dollars and the film to start with. First we are going to show the picture in New York, in some Hungarian hall. We will make money on that, and then we will start touring every city where we can find enough Hungarians to make up an audience. I need somebody to project the picture, somebody to rent the halls, somebody to take care of the advertising in the papers, and there will be plenty of work for the others in taking care of the film to see that it is always in good condition, and many other things. Each of us will share equally in the profits. And the profits ought to be tremendous. I have everything figured out. What do you say?"

By that time I was very much interested. Bandi had no job, and I was a clerk in a United Cigar store. It was a permanent job, but it suddenly looked gray and dismal. Perhaps there was not much future in the cigar business, after all, and who wanted to be a clerk for a lifetime? This film business was different. We could make money in a few months. The film would be successful, no doubt of that. We could charge fifty cents admission. If only one thousand people came to see the performance, we could clear five hundred dollars. But if we were to play for three days in one place, that would be fifteen hundred dollars, and how many places there were in America! If I stayed with United, I could make about ninety dollars a month and be bored to death. With the film I could make that much money in a day with little or no work. And think of the adventure! Almost anything could happen on the road. New people, new faces, and an interesting and colorful life! And then the money! I could make enough money to go home for a visit . . . and perhaps stay there for good.

Home again, to see my darling father and mother . . . my friends . . . Klari . . . Home! Should I be a coward and keep a steady but unimportant job for years? I looked at Bandi. I could see eagerness and interest in the proposition on his face.

"Well, what do you think about it?" Alexej asked.

"I rather like the idea. I think we'll go with you. It will be great to travel and make money in such a pleasant way."

Alexej shook hands with us. It was decided.

The next day I wrote a letter to my manager, explaining that I had a very good offer and would not work for the United Cigar Stores any more.

That same day we started to work in our new business. In two weeks we planned to have our first performance. We did not have to pay for the advertisements in advance. . . .

We only needed enough money to keep us alive until the performance. Alexej had one hundred dollars, and I had a little money also.

At the first performance, the big hall we had rented was not full, but still the first performance was quite a success. The net profit was three hundred dollars. It happened that the picture appeared on the screen upside down a few times, and once the machine stopped for no reason at all. The film was not in the best condition, and broke once or twice during the performance, but still it was a success.

However, New Yorkers were too sophisticated. Nothing was good enough for them. We expected to make the big money in the smaller cities. It was hard to leave Yelena, to leave New York, but opportunity was knocking at the door.

In the small places near New York, the film was not as big a hit as we thought it would be, and at one place the audience even booed. But still we made some money. Frank and John became discouraged in Passaic, New Jersey, and went back to New York.

Alexej, Bandi, and myself kept on in spite of everything. One had to fight for success, we agreed. Three of us were enough to do all the work, and the money we made was divided only among three people, instead of five, which made quite a difference.

We struggled along bravely and went as far as Detroit. We had great faith in that city. People were prosperous there because of the great factories. There were also many Hungarians living in Detroit, and we were sure we would be successful.

However, contrary to our hopes, the first performance turned out so very badly that we decided not to show the film anymore in that city. Bandi suggested that we should drop the whole thing. It was no use going on. Somehow people were not interested in the picture, and it would be better to quit the business altogether.

We counted our money. We had exactly seventy dollars, thirty dollars less than we had started with.

"It is not enough for all of us to go back," Bandi said sadly.

"One of us can go, though. There is enough money for one person to return to New York," I said.

Bandi understood my meaning immediately. Alexej's sweetheart was in New York. Alexej must be the one to go back. We could stay in Detroit and try out our luck there. Bandi turned to Alexej.

"I think you should go back alone. We are going to stay here. You can take sixty dollars and leave us ten. That will be enough for us."

"No," Alexej said, "we are going to divide this money, it is only fair. And I am going to stay with you."

Bandi was very determined at times. This was one of those times.

"You are in love with that girl in New York, Alexej, and you are going back to her immediately."

Alexej did not answer.

We took him to the station and saw him off.

CHAPTER 28

ALTHOUGH DETROIT WAS absolutely strange to us, we both succeeded in getting jobs that same day. I became the inevitable busboy, and Bandi got a job as the captain in a large restaurant. Tall and handsome, he was a perfect fit for his job. He made twenty-five dollars a week, and I made fifteen. Both of us had our meals in our places of employment.

I was determined to keep my job, and Bandi held his easily without any effort. We were not interested in our work; we were not interested in anything. We had both caught a dangerous sickness at the same time. It came suddenly, while we were reading a Hungarian newspaper. We were homesick, and as the days passed, the desire to return to Budapest grew and grew.

We did things for our living with mechanical gestures; we said words without meaning anything, and every minute of the day we wanted to go home. We wanted to see our people again. Nostalgia is a strange thing. We wanted to see the very stones of the streets that we once walked on; the houses, the signs, the familiar faces; and, above all, to find our younger selves that we had left behind.

Of course I had pictured my return home differently. A big, luxurious car and the chauffeur waiting outside on the street, in front of the apartment house. . . . But what could

I do? My uncle had said years ago in Budapest that miners in America wore silk shirts and rode in their own cars. Yes, perhaps miners did, but not I.

Nevertheless, the only thing to do was to go home, beaten and humble, but home. It seemed that I could not keep on struggling anymore. Life and success in America were for strong men, and—let's be frank—for better men than I.

Bandi and I dreamed and planned every night. That is what kept us alive. I used to go to the railway station to see the trains leave. Trains were coming and going constantly. Trains were lovely. One could go places on them, one could go anywhere.

One thousand dollars! That was the amount we needed for both of us to leave. It was a hopelessly large amount; but perhaps we could save it in two or three years if we could stand it that long.

One night, about three o'clock, when Bandi came home from work, he woke me up and asked, "How much money do you have?"

I looked at him sleepily. It was a stupid question to ask at three in the morning, but I answered good-naturedly, "Three dollars."

"I have seven," he said.

I sat up in bed and looked at him. He was pale and in the half-dark room; his eyes shone like lights. He seemed very excited.

"What is this all about?" I asked him.

"Those damned waiters have driven me crazy. They were talking about nothing all day but a certain gambling house they go to after work. It is open day and night. Some of them lose, some of them win; but last night Jack, a waiter at our place, won two thousand dollars. Everything was over in half an hour. He started with thirty. We have ten dollars now. It doesn't make much difference whether we have it or not. Let's go there, now, and try our luck. Maybe something will happen. Maybe we can go home if we are lucky."

I immediately became excited myself. I jumped quickly out of bed, and in a minute I was dressed, ready to go.

We did not say a word to each other on the way to the gambling house. We were afraid to talk. We reached the building. From the outside it did not look very promising; it was old and deserted. No lights were visible.

We went through many doors, and finally stepped into a small room. A tough-looking individual made us stand on a stool, and he went through our pockets thoroughly, examining even our hats in search for weapons. I had to smile at the idea of our carrying revolvers.

We climbed a flight of stairs, and wherever we went, we noticed little holes in the walls and ceilings, and through these holes, eyes peeped at us, watching our every movement.

A little door at the end of the stairs opened by itself, and we found ourselves in the gambling room. It was a large room, containing many green, covered tables, around which people from all walks of life formed circles. At each table a man was throwing dice. There were four or five men perched on high stools looking down on the people and watching the games. I saw piles of money on the tables; the man who ran each game carried a large roll of bills, and before him he had several hundred silver dollars.

The people in the gambling house were talking in terms I had never heard before. I heard them say "seven and eleven," "hard four," "come home to Daddy," and other mysterious expressions.

Bandi knew something of the game from his waiter friend, so he gave me all the money he had, saying, "The less you know, the better it is. Everything is just a matter of luck."

I went to one of the tables. I looked to see what the others were doing. There were numbers on the table, and people put money in different places. I put our ten dollars on a certain number. The attendant asked me something, but I could not understand what he said. I did not want to appear green at the game, so I just nodded my head. I remembered from the movies that if anybody won at casino, the croupier gave the money to the winner with a little rakelike instrument. Nobody raked me any money, so I understood that I had lost the ten dollars. Somehow it did not bother me at all.

The people around the table were much more interesting to me than the whole game, of which I knew nothing. I saw all types. Well-dressed, dignified men who trembled and perspired as they lost small amounts; men in rags and worn-out shoes losing thousands and thousands of dollars that they had just won a moment before. Faces were crimson. Everybody was excited and talking to himself.

The croupier seemed to be the only sane person in the whole crowd. All the others were crazy. The whole scene again reminded me of the jail.

Hearing a gasp from Bandi, I turned to him and saw that his eyes were staring, his mouth was open, and streams of perspiration were flowing from his face. He gasped for breath, looked down at the table, and with a great effort, cried, "Take it away!"

As I looked down in the direction he was staring, I saw some bills, and by instinct I understood what he meant. Slowly I reached for the money, momentarily expecting somebody to hit my hand . . . but nobody did. I took the money. It was mine! I understood that the ten dollars had multiplied at a beautiful rate. I had let it lie there, not knowing that I had won at every turn, from the minute I had first laid the money down. I did not count the winnings, although I saw twenty dollar bills in the roll.

I immediately put some more money on the same number, watching it constantly, as if hypnotized. It disappeared in a minute. Evidently I had lost it. Some more money. I had won; then I lost again. Then I won and won and won. And I continued putting money on the very same spot, mechanically, like a maniac. Bandi was tugging at my coat. I turned to him furiously. His face was distorted.

"Paul, stop it! For God's sake, stop it!" he hissed. I felt like killing him.

"You are crazy! Let me alone!" I answered through clenched teeth.

He grabbed what money he could, and I let him take it. I kept on playing.

Then Bandi came back and whispered to me, "Paul, it's five hundred. Please come immediately. You'll lose it all!"

He gave me a look. Was I insane? Should I leave? I played and played, and felt a terrible pain creeping into my brain. It was a shooting pain, and for a moment I could not see. At that very moment Bandi dragged me away.

In the hall we stopped and counted the money, and then I realized for the first time what had happened. The pain miraculously disappeared, and an indescribable and unbelievable happiness took possession of me. We had nine hundred and eighty-six dollars to go home with. Europe! Budapest!

I thought of my mother immediately. I would not telegraph or write; just ring the bell at home, and my mother would fall into my arms as she saw me.

Bandi and I danced as we went home. . . . We jumped and yelled from happiness. We were content. We had everything.

Near the building we lived in, two men were coming from the opposite direction. Bandi happily said to me, "Maybe I know them. I wish I could tell them what has happened. I feel I must tell somebody."

The men came nearer and suddenly I saw a large revolver in front of my nose and heard a sharp, short sentence:

"Stick 'em up, boys. Don't say a word, or I'll . . ."

I lifted my arms. The man went through my pockets and took the money from me. I could not understand what was happening. Bandi was limp as we made our way to our room. The money was gone. . . . Bandi threw himself down on the bed and started to sob. I tried to console him, and then cried with him.

CHAPTER 29

THE WORK IN the restaurant went on just as usual, though we did not have much energy. We tried to forget the whole nightmare.

I wanted to hold on to my job. I was saving money and did not want to give up the idea of going home. I did not write to Yelena, because I did not want her to know how unhappy I was. I was not in the mood to lie to her.

One day a well-dressed, middle-aged man came into our restaurant. As he sat down at a table, I went to get a glass of water for him. As I was about to put the water on the table, I noticed that he had taken a cigarette from his pocket and was looking for a match. I was too eager to serve him. I wanted to light the cigarette and give him the water at the same time. The result was that I spilled the whole glass of ice-cold water on his well-pressed trousers.

The gentleman was very angry. His face turned crimson, and he raised his clenched fist as if to strike me. Evidently he had a very bad temper. However, he did not get violent; he called the manager over, and demanded my immediate discharge from the restaurant. He was a highly respected guest and I wasn't such a desirable busboy, so he won the case. I was fired on the spot. The manager paid me the money that was coming to me; I took off the white uniform and left the place. The man who had caused all my troubles was ready to leave at the same time. How different our departures were!

On the street we even went in the same direction. God knows how different our destinations were, but just the same we traveled on the same road. I was depressed, but I had a sort of I-don't-care-what-is-going-to-happen feeling. It was my usual reaction on losing a job.

We looked at each other, and I saw in his kind eyes that he felt sorry for me. By that time we were walking next to each other. I spoke to him.

"You see, sir, you won. And now I have lost my job. I really did not mean to spill water on you. I am very sorry. I must admit, though, that I am not very handy as a busboy."

The stranger was silent for a moment, but the silence was not hostile. Then he said, "I have a very bad temper. I am sorry, too, but I think I can get you another job in some restaurant. I know many people."

"Thanks," I answered, "but it's no use. I will lose that job, too. You should not recommend me for any job. I am not a busboy, really.

"What is your profession? Perhaps I can help you."

"Nothing. . . . I have no profession whatsoever. I am not a shoemaker, not a plumber, not a dentist, not a carpenter. I am just a greenhorn, that is all."

"Your English isn't bad at all. How long have you been in this country?"

"A few years," I answered. "But that isn't it. I am a greenhorn and I shall remain one. I just cannot succeed in anything. I am a failure. True enough, I had one year at the university in Budapest. I was an excellent student. I wanted to be a doctor, but things went wrong. I came to America, and now I am a nobody. Not even a busboy."

"But, my son," he said sympathetically, "how can you talk like that? You are young, and an intelligent man. You can do great things in America still. You must choose some profession and stick to it. You don't have to be a greenhorn all your life. You can make a man out of yourself if you will only try. I am willing to help you. Here is my card. I have to go now. Come and look me up some day. Perhaps I can be of some assistance to you. Goodbye."

CHAPTER 30

FIGURES, FIGURES, MACHINES, checks, and more figures. I was working in a bank. The kindhearted man on whom I had spilled water in the restaurant had turned out to be the manager of a bank. I had looked him up, and he had told me that he could use a Hungarian because his branch was located in the Hungarian section. My salary was one hundred and fifty dollars a month.

They liked me at the bank. The manager told me I had a great future in the banking business. Someday I would be the manager of this branch, and later on, perhaps, something much better.

I was not homesick anymore. Maybe fate chose not to let us go home on money that was not earned honestly. It had been shameful to be ready to admit defeat. We would have to try again. It was fate again that had made me spill water on my present employer.

Yes, fate was strange. One could never figure it out. It was no use to speculate and calculate; one had just to accept everything without questioning. For was it not fate that Klari had married Charley, my very best friend, whose idea it was to go to America, and who had left me in so cowardly a manner in Trieste? He had teased me into the American idea, and had left me and married the girl I loved. Klari wrote me saying that they were very happy. As I read the letter I watched myself, and was surprised to see that neither did I take it badly nor was I even terribly unhappy about it. I had never suspected that I would take the loss of her so easily. It almost hurt me that I could not be unhappy and desperate about her. But life was striding on swiftly, and she, the dear little girl, was left behind somewhere. I had lost her long ago. My life had run away from her and the zoo and the soda stand. So Charley had married her. Well, God give them all happiness. . . . He was a liar, true, but a nice one. I wanted them to be happy, for I looked at him as one who had taken my place, the place of my cowardly self.

I would not be going home for a while yet. Eventually I would be a successful banker, a financier; and then the great limousine would maybe be a reality, after all.

I was old enough by that time to know and understand things better. Bandi had the same opinion regarding things. He no longer wanted to go home with five hundred dollars, just a little more than the price of the ticket. He would stay, too. We were young, and determined to try and try again. Nothing was lost.

I was very careful to keep my job. In a little while I received a raise, and the customers all said they liked to deal with me at the bank. They told me all their troubles, all their joys, and I patiently listened and gave them advice.

The manager was a peculiar man. He was disgusted at heart while talking politely to people who had small accounts, and he actually disliked those whose accounts were overdrawn; and he was right. People should be clever enough to make money, I thought, for money is the most important thing in life. Money is respect, comfort, luxury, everything. One must be strong, one must have willpower, one must make money. Some day I would be the manager of this branch, and then I would go higher and higher.

My father would be satisfied with me. It would be nice to have a rich banker for a son. I would have money and a beautiful mansion to live in and people would point me out on the street, saying, with awe in their hearts, "There goes the young banker!"

Through my bank connections I became acquainted with a man who was the stage manager of a theatre company in Detroit. I talked to him about Bandi, and told him I would send him around and perhaps he might give him a job as an actor. Bandi was more successful than I thought he would be. The manager hired him with a very pleasant salary and many chances for advancement. Bandi would make good, I was sure. The stage manager, the director, and his fellow actors liked him and helped him.

Life was not exciting, however. I was rather calm, and I always had enough money. Bandi was content also. We shared a place and planned to do important things, to be successful no matter how hard it might be. And it was not so hard. I worked every day, but it was a clean, manly work, and I was proud of my profession. People learned to respect me as a banker.

Finally, I thought, my life was on the right track. Success was within my reach!

The weeks passed slowly and I worked happily every day. I was glad I had finally settled down. Gone were the days of busboying, hunger, and homelessness. I came to the conclusion that fate wanted me to be successful in spite of myself.

I had had to struggle and wander so much only to know and appreciate a quiet and peaceful life when I met it. No more walks on rainy nights for me. No sir, that belonged to the past. Of course, I was young, I had not known better; and one must go through a lot of experiences while one is young. It was good for a person. It made one strong and gave one perseverance, a basis, so to speak.

Oh, life was simple for me. I was putting away money every week and would get a raise of a certain amount every few months. Nothing could happen. I was going to become a successful banker, with a car and a house, eventually, and would be an upright and successful citizen of Detroit. I would probably marry the daughter of a banker, a nice daughter, for there is no reason why a rich girl should not be good-looking too. A straight road, perfectly straight. No one could throw a monkey wrench into the machinery of my life anymore. I was finally and definitely on the road that led to a worthy life. Thank God!

CHAPTER 31

After a long time I received a letter from Yelena. We had not written to each other for three or four months. I led a settled, quiet life; I did not need her.

My eyes opened wide with surprise as I saw the postmark on the letter before I opened it. Hollywood! Yelena, in Hollywood?

Bandi's face turned red with excitement as I read the letter aloud:

Paul, Paul, Paul, yes, I am in Hollywood, gorgeous, darling Hollywood! I can hardly tell you how it happened. . . . When I finally decided to come here . . . I was sad and tired in New York, sad for weeks and weeks. My work bored me. . . . More than that, it actually pained me. I suddenly realized how futile and stupid my life was: to start every blessed day by describing some murder, and then go through the day writing articles on politics and prohibition and scandals. And doing the same thing over and over again for years, and receiving the same certain salary every month, and living in the same surroundings all the time. I just couldn't do it any longer. One day the yearning for diversion possessed me so strongly that I felt like screaming, like crying out loud that I wouldn't do it any longer; and immediately, on the spur of the moment, I went to the editor's office and resigned. And then I cried from happiness, for I felt that a new life had started for me: a better, more worthy life, an exciting, uncertain life. I packed my wardrobe and books, and here I am, a happy resident of Hollywood.

I want to thank you for this, Paul, because unconsciously you have made me do this. I have seen your years, how much more rich, how much more complete they have been than my stale, cobwebby existence. I felt an irresistible yearning to taste life at its fullest; to step out of the routine, out of the endless line for cake and live the life of youth: to fight, to struggle, to dream, and to plan—even if it never brings results. Everybody says I have been foolish, and perhaps I have. But it is delicious to be foolish.

What am I going to do here? I don't know, and that is the beauty of it. I do not know. . . . I do not know. . . . I keep on repeating that magic sentence. Shall I live in a dinky, furnished room? Or a sweet, Spanish bungalow? I don't know. Shall I become a scenario writer? Or an actress? Or a starving Hollywood dreamer? I don't know and I am happy that I don't. Now I am the greenhorn.

The geranium—which we claim as a Hungarian flower, and which thrives on a single little stem in pots, in Hungarian peasant homes—blossoms here wild, and grows as tall as I. I adore it! Garages are covered with myriads of roses. Flowers grow on the edges of sidewalks, belonging to nobody and everybody. Red and blue window frames. People in heavy make-up and funny costumes on the streets. . . .

Oh, Paul, try to understand me. I envied you for that blessed uncertainty that gave value to your every tomorrow. I wanted to taste it, I wanted to get drunk with it once in my life, and it does not matter how much I pay for it. I'll die just the same.

I am indebted already to Hollywood for the happiness of the first few days; the thrills and joy of it. I am willing to pay for it . . . gladly.

I am pleased that you are finally settled and are about to graduate from the greenhorn class. You had a little bit too much of struggling, I think. Yes, you doubly deserve a little comfort and security. Do not begrudge the suffering you endured! It will make a better man out of you. I am certain you will be successful. And when you are a respected and well-to-do banker, with money and a house and a car in your name, will you associate with such a nobody as I might be?

I am too happy to write a detailed description of everything. Will write again in a few days. My love to Bandi, and my everlasting gratitude to you, ex-greenhorn of mine, for showing me my shackles.

Yelena

After I read the letter, Bandi and I did not speak a word to each other for several hours. But that night, in the dark, Bandi said, "I think Yelena was really foolish to leave her comfortable life and plunge into the uncertainty of Hollywood."

"I think so, too," I answered. "It was really very foolish . . . very, very, foolish."

I did not sleep much that night. I was sorry for Yelena. She would have a hard life there. No such calamity could happen to me. I was settled for life. I had two hundred dollars in the bank, and my account was growing steadily.

I did not think that I would ever leave Detroit. After all, it was a nice city. But there was no reason why I shouldn't go to the railway station occasionally. Bandi came, too. It was so nice to linger there together for an hour or so. Trains were coming and going. Trains from all parts of the country. And to all parts of the country.

Yelena is in Hollywood. . . . The climate is notoriously fine there. Hollywood is a nice city.

Besides my good salary, I wrote letters for people and did other odd jobs that earned me money on the side. I had several good suits, shirts, a tuxedo, and three pairs of shoes, good ones.

The cage in the bank, in any bank, is just like a jail. Of course one doesn't have to remain a prisoner. I was free. It was of my own free will that I went to work every morning; nobody forced me to go behind the bars. After my workday was done I was free but, being tired, I went to bed early to be able to get up early again in the morning. Bank managers—as a rule—are stupid people. Somehow they are gray; they lead dull lives, involved in checks, money, and customers.

I loved to see the trains going.

Money is success. Money is the most important thing in life.

Maybe something was wrong with my health. There were no definite symptoms I could describe to a doctor, but I was ever in the grips of a generally bad mood. I did not have much of an appetite, and in Detroit the winters were cold, with people dying of pneumonia and flu, or freezing to death, every year.

Perhaps I needed a change in climate.

In Hollywood the climate is lovely. California has the best climate on earth. Yes, practically the best. No exaggerating that.

Hollywood is a nice city . . . the center of the world. The most interesting people live there; actors, actresses, writers, rich people, poor people, everybody who amounts to anything in this world lives in

Hollywood. One could do big things there. Bandi would have a marvelous chance there. He would make good as an actor. His stage experience would help him a lot, too. He would have opportunity, unlimited opportunity.

One night both Bandi and I were in very low spirits, and I started to talk to him.

"Detroit is a very boring city to live in. I don't know, but this place is getting on my nerves. Always the same . . . always the same places . . . the same people. . . . We ought to do something about it."

"Listen, Paul," Bandi said after a long silence, "have you ever seen geraniums growing as tall as Yelena?"

"No," I answered. "Why do you ask?"

Bandi spoke nonchalantly.

"No reason. I just wanted to know. No reason at all. . . ."

We decided to go for a walk. Though Bandi was not very enthusiastic about it, I insisted.

"I just read in the paper that there is no starvation in California at all," I said, "for the poor people can eat fruit."

"Really? Oh, I love fruit, especially oranges."

"I do too. I am just dying for an orange."

We were just passing by a market that had lots of oranges.

"To pick them from the tree," I continued, "must be marvelous."

Bandi wanted to turn away from Woodward Avenue, but I stopped him, surprised:

"Where are you going?" I asked him. "This is the way to the nearest Western Union office."

And after taking a deep sigh of relief, I started to hum a song. Bandi put his arm around my shoulder and, with a wink, he joined in.

After we sent a telegram to Yelena, notifying her that we were leaving for Hollywood on the next train, Bandi said, "But we are going to be greenhorns again."

"Ah, who wants to be a banker?" I answered. "I hate figures, and I don't want to spend my life in a cage."

Bandi understood.

"Of course not. You are not a criminal. It is ridiculous."

It was ridiculous, for we started to laugh, and we laughed while packing our things. Even on the train, Hollywood–bound, we continued to roar and shriek and scream with laughter.

The passengers were shocked.

THE END

Also Available

My First Two Hundred Years
An autobiography by Pál Királyhegyi

(Paul King)

IN HIS AUTOBIOGRAPHY, *My First Two Hundred Years*, the writer's whole life story is recounted with the same subtle humor found in *Greenhorn.*

Initially published in 1979 in Hungarian, and for the first time in English in 2017.

In the early years of the twentieth century, Királyhegyi, a young Hungarian, stowed away on a ship bound for America. He by turns worked as a busboy, elevator operator, and banker until he boarded a train for Hollywood. There, he realized his American dream and wrote films, hobnobbing with the likes of Charlie Chaplin. But while at the height of his success, the restless Királyhegyi, known in America as Paul King, decided to return to Europe. As a Jew, the writer was "just in time" to be deported to a string of concentration camps in World War II Germany. Ultimately, Királyhegyi was liberated by the US Armed Forces and returned to Hungary to withstand the Soviet occupation and flourish in Budapest as a playwright and novelist.

Certainly no other writer has experienced the golden era of Hollywood, the ghastliness of the Holocaust, and the absurdity of Communism first-hand, and chronicled them with such a breezy wit uncorrupted by cynicism or bitterness.

Heart-rending and inspirational, a rare life-story that is also a page-turner, it's the type of book young and old will be able to enjoy and learn from.

Coming In 2018

Not Everyone Has Died

Pál Királyhegyi

Királyhegyi published his absorbing memoir of the Holocaust *Not Everyone Has Died* in Hungary in 1947. A huge hit in his home country, it remained unavailable in English until now.

An English-language version was planned in 1947 but tight control by the Hungarian Communist Party over postwar Hungarian cultural life made its publication impossible.

Although Királyhegyi incorporated a version of it into his 1979 autobiography *My First Two Hundred Years, Not Everyone Has Died* deserves to be published on its own due to its importance as a stunning historical document, and also to present the original, full text to Királyhegyi's English language readers.

Seventy-one years after its first publication, we are proud to present *Not Everyone Has Died* to an English-speaking readership.

About The Author

Pál Királyhegyi (pron. Pahl Keer-rye-hedyee; AKA Paul King, 1900–1981) was a Hungarian writer, journalist, humorist, TV personality, and screenwriter and perhaps the most quotable Hungarian of the twentieth century. He was the author of several novels and books of nonfiction. As he relates in *Greenhorn* and, later, in *My First Two Hundred Years,* in 1920 he and a fellow Hungarian stowed away on a ship bound for New York City. There, after years of hardship, hard work, and adventures aplenty, they moved to Hollywood and began working in the film industry. His friend went on to become a major director under the Americanized name Charles Vidor, while Királyhegyi wrote this autobiographical novel *Greenhorn,* published under the pseudonym Paul King. In 1931, homesick, he moved back to Hungary, where he worked as a journalist and theatre critic. In 1938 he moved to England, where he worked for the *Daily Telegraph* and in the film industry and remained until 1941. He returned again to Hungary, only to eventually be sent to an internal labor camp, and before long, in 1944, to Auschwitz and other concentration camps, where he nearly perished. After he was liberated by the US Armed Forces, in 1945 he returned to Budapest, where he wrote pieces for cabaret theatres. As a writer and an intellectual who had lived abroad, he found it increasingly difficult to find work after Hungary became a one-party, communist state, and in 1951 he was sent to the countryside for a time in internal exile. One of many quotes attributed to Királyhegyi: “He who has a sense of humor knows everything. He who doesn’t is capable of anything.”

www.ingramcontent.com/pod-product-compliance
Lightning Source LLC
Chambersburg PA
CBHW022112040426
42450CB00006B/666
9780999158708